Poisonous & Hallucinogenic
MUSHROOMS
2ND EDITION

Richard & Karen Haard

Illustrations by Cindy Davis
Photography by
Lee Mann & Richard Haard

Homestead Book Company
Seattle
1980

Published by:

Homestead Book Company
4009 Stoneway North,
Seattle, Washington
98103

ISBN 0-930180-05-4

Printed in the U.S.A.

1st Edition:
   1st Printing September 1975
2nd Edition:
   1st Printing January 1977
   2nd Printing June 1978
   3rd Printing June 1980

This book may be ordered from the Publisher. Send the
cover price of the book plus $1.00 for shipping and handling.

Contents

Introduction

A mushroom book only about those fungi which will make you ill, or bring about your death, seems unlikely to be popular with readers. However, the 1st edition of this book has proved the contrary. The overwhelming public response to this book has provided us with the impetus to provide periodic updating of the text.

This book offers for the first time complete information on both poisonous and hallucinogenic mushrooms. It should be useful to the physician who wishes to diagnose and treat mushroom poisoning and to the lay person who wishes to avoid poisoning. This book is also of use to the person who wishes to use mushrooms for inducing altered states of consciousness. We feel that avoiding this latter group would be akin to burying one's head in the sand since thousands of people are now tramping lawns and pastures in search of the elusive magic mushrooms. Consumption of these mushrooms has become a worldwide phenomenon, with interest being shown on every continent of the globe (excepting possibly Antarctica) in using mushrooms as an intoxicant.

We are concerned about indiscriminate use of these powerful hallucinogenic materials and have attempted to present and foster an open, mature attitude towards them. As mushroom toxicology consultants at our local hospital, we have seen cases of mushroom poisoning in persons who were collecting both for the pot and the head. For this reason we feel it is essential that we include methods for identification of all major poisonous and hallucinogenic mushrooms. Field features are emphasized but, where necessary, microscopic features are utilized. Simple laboratory chromatographic tests for diagnosis of some principal toxins are also included. Once you read through this section, you will understand that the written text serves as an aid to guide your eye to the distinctive features of each mushroom. By faithfully checking these distinctive features, identification should be assured.

A companion volume to this book is available, entitled *Foraging for Edible Wild Mushrooms.*

2

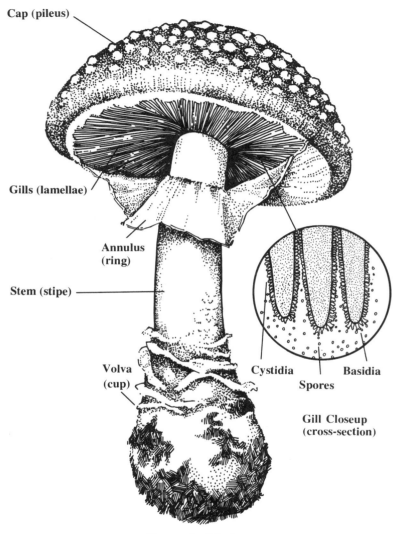

Cap (pileus)

Gills (lamellae)

Annulus
(ring)

Stem (stipe)

Volva
(cup)

Cystidia

Spores

Basidia

Gill Closeup
(cross-section)

Plate 1—Parts of a Mushroom

What is a Mushroom?

Mushrooms which appear after a warm rain are a more obvious minority of fungi. The fungi are a large and diverse group of organisms which range from thread-like molds in rotting leaves and supermarket sweet potatoes to conspicuous brackets and mushrooms. The latter category are only organs of reproduction for organisms which live within wood, soil, or roots of living trees. In order to appreciate the role of a mushroom as a component in the life history of a fungus, let's follow the life history of a typical example, *Psilocybe cubensis*.

The natural habitat of our mushroom is on dung and decaying vegetation in most semi-tropical regions of the world. The mushroom develops very rapidly after a rainy spell so that it can mature and shed its crop of spores before the sun dries up its precious moisture. Once the mushroom reaches the button stage, development is complete, even though the gills are enclosed within a protective sheath beneath the unexpanded cap. In this stage the young *Psilocybe* awaits a fresh supply of moisture and, with an afternoon shower, develops into a full grown mushroom by the following morning. This rapid development is brought about by the sudden uptake of water by the vegetative mycelium and an expansion of each cell of the mushroom. As the stem grows longer under the surge of water pressure, the cap begins to expand, breaking the protective veil which covers the gills.

A purple stain which can be observed on the stem is actually direct evidence of spores that developed on the surface of the gills. These arise from club-like microscopic structures called basidia which bear four pegs. Upon each peg sits a spore (basidiospore) which receives from the mother basidium some cell sap, stored food, and a haploid nucleus. This spore with its haploid nucleus is analogous to the human egg or sperm. When the proper stage of maturity is reached and the moisture supply is adequate, the spores are forcibly flicked away, in rapid succession from the basidium, a distance approximately half the space between the gills. This procedure of spore production and release is repeated 1 to 5 billion times a day in an average mushroom.

Spores released during calm conditions such as the early morning hours tend to settle in a mass at the base of the mushroom, failing to survive. During daylight hours the free spore, floating among the other aerial plankton, is protected by a darkly pigmented wall which screens out the sun's deadly ultraviolet rays but, even so, the elements take their toll of these reproductive cells. Spores may drift hundreds or thousands of miles, but they are eventually brought back to earth by attachment to raindrops or by being caught in a becalmed air space.

Once our fungal *voyageur* has recontacted earth, it can begin to grow when adequate moisture is present. Using stored food reserves, the tiny spore produces a simple vegetative growth which seeks nutriment. Many dung-loving fungi must actually pass through the gut of an animal before growing. Thus spores landing on grass are automatically placed in a meadow muffin.

The organism has now begun growth and assimilation, but must find a mate in order to produce new mushrooms. Some fungi are self-compatible (i.e., they can mate with themselves) but most require more complicated matching. Only at this point can the fungus proceed to its sexually reproductive stage, the mushroom.

Plate 2—Life Cycle of a Mushroom

How to Use This Guide

Positively identifying an unknown mushroom as edible, poisonous, or hallucinogenic can be difficult. It is even more difficult when only cooked remains or stomach contents are available. In the latter case only microscopic or chemical tests or symptomatic studies of the patient can be used. If you are interested in avoiding becoming a mushroom poisoning patient it behooves you to use the following guidelines as a course of study.

1. Each mushroom has its own distinctive habitat and season; learn them in order to know where and when to collect.

2. Go out and collect mushrooms at least once a week. Even more often than that is better.

3. Using the techniques outlined in this first section, work on your unknown mushrooms during the one or two days after your collecting.

4. During the early stages of learning to identify mushrooms, remember it is not as important to name all mushrooms as it is to learn to discriminate. Take notes on all collections and even develop your own personal names until the scientific name is discovered.

5. With time you will add new names to your vocabulary, slowly but constantly. You may notice that as you spend more time with mushrooms your sharpened powers of perception allow you to notice additional details.

6. When comparing your unknown mushroom to a description in this text, every feature must be positively demonstrated. Once this is done you should be able to identify any mushroom which is listed in this manual.

Identifying Unknown Mushrooms

Let's assume that at this point you have been out and collected a basket of mushrooms.

On arriving home, unwrap all of your specimens on a large table and sort them according to your perception of size, form and colour. How many apparent duplicate collections do you have? Sort out ten of the nicest specimens which represent the full range of size, shape, and colour and do the following:

1. Set up a spore print.

2. Write a simple description of each mushroom, and include habitat and substrate (e.g., in Douglas fir forest on wood).

3. Give each specimen a temporary name (e.g., pinkish one with yellow gills).

4. Number each specimen, rewrap, and store in the vegetable crisper of your refrigerator until the spore prints are completed.

5. Once the spore prints are completed, sort out your collections into groups which you perceive are different.

6. Now—using the following plates and terms as a guide, write a complete description of each specimen. **Note:** Be sure to study 4-5 specimens of each collection in order to understand variability within the species. You will find these notes are quite useful when refreshing your memory at a later date.

Many of the terms listed and illustrated in this section may not be used in the text of this book. They are included to give a complete reference to the mushroom terminology used in highly technical literature.

Descriptive Terms

I. Fruiting body (entire mushroom)

a. Type (plate 3)—branched, clitocyboid, collybioid, cup-shaped, globose, mycenoid, pleurotoid, pluteoid, stellate, stipitate-pileate, tricholomoid.

b. Position—above ground or subterranean.

7

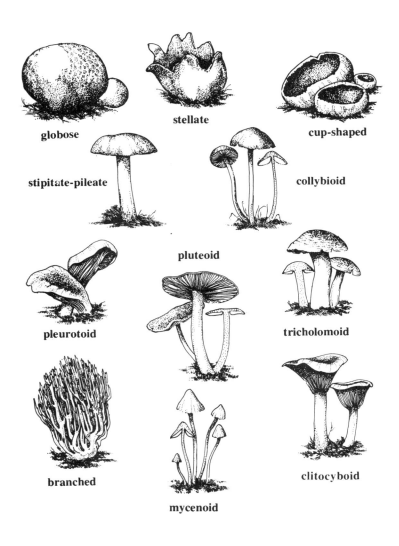

globose

stellate

cup-shaped

stipitate-pileate

collybioid

pluteoid

pleurotoid

tricholomoid

branched

mycenoid

clitocyboid

Plate 3—Fruiting Body

8

II. Cap (pileus)

a. Overall shape (plate 4)—brain-like (convoluted), campanulate, conchate, conic, convex; coralloid, dimidiate, infundibuliform, ovoid, pendulous, petaloid, plane, resupinate, saddle-shaped, spatulate, sub-globose, umbilicate, umbonate, ungulate.

b. Shape central portion (plate 5)—cuspidate, depressed, mammiform, subumbonate, truncate, umbilicate, umbonate.

c. Shape marginal portion (plate 5)—appressed, incurved, involute, recurved, revolute, rounded, straight.

d. Surface texture (plate 6)—fibrillose-scaly, floccose, furfuraceous (mealy), glabrous, hirsute, hispid, hygrophanous, plicate-striate, rimose-areolate, silky, squamulose, squarrose, striate, strigose, subpruinose, subtomentose, villose, zonate.

e. Cuticle (skin of cap) (plate 5)—cellular, fibrous, filamentous, hymeniform, palisade-like, separable or inseparable.

f. Trama (flesh of cap or context) (plate 5)—colour, colour changes with bruising, consistency, odour, taste where safe, thick or thin.

III. Gills (lamellae)

a. Pattern (plate 7)—anastomosed or forked.

b. Spacing (plate 7)—crowded, distant, incomplete, subdistant.

c. Shape in cross-section (plate 7)—acute, ridgiform, rounded, straight, truncate.

d. Relation to stem (plate 7)—adnate, adnexed, decurrent, emarginate, free, seceding, subfree.

e. Edge (plate 7)—crenate, crenulate, dentate, entire, serrate.

f. Width (cross-section) (plate 8)—thick, thin. Depth (top to bottom)—broad, narrow.

g. Relation to cap trama (plate 8)—nonseparable or separable.

h. Texture (plate 8)—autodeliquescent, fragile, waxy.

i. Trama (context) (plate 8)—bilateral (divergent), inverse (convergent), parallel (regular), interwoven (intermixed).

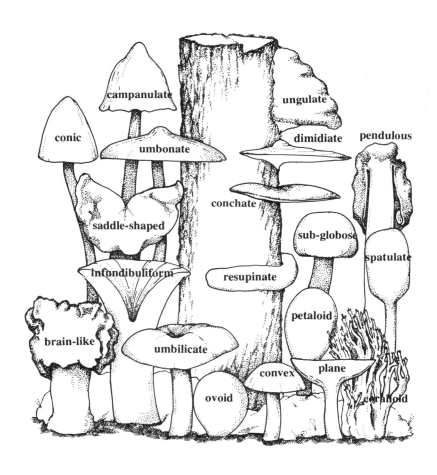

Plate 4—Overall Cap Shapes

10

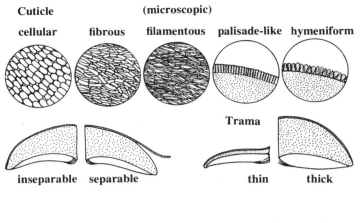

Cuticle — (microscopic)

cellular — fibrous — filamentous — palisade-like — hymeniform

Trama

inseparable — separable — thin — thick

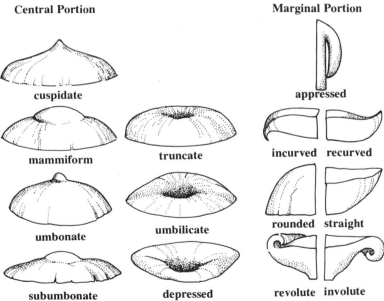

Central Portion

cuspidate

mammiform — truncate

umbonate — umbilicate

subumbonate — depressed

Marginal Portion

appressed

incurved — recurved

rounded — straight

revolute — involute

Plate 5—Cap Shapes, Cuticles and Tramas

11

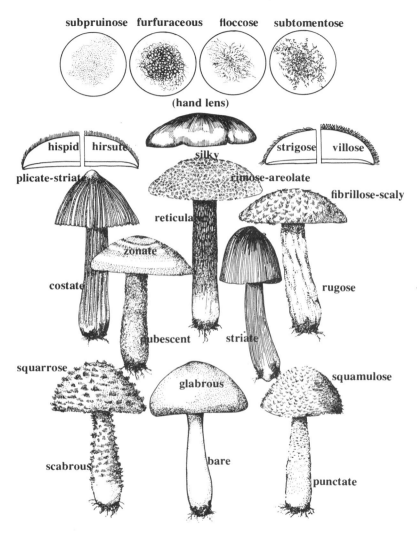

subpruinose furfuraceous floccose subtomentose

(hand lens)

hispid hirsute silky strigose villose

plicate-striate rimose-areolate

fibrillose-scaly

reticulate

zonate

costate rugose

pubescent striate

squarrose squamulose

glabrous

scabrous bare punctate

Plate 6—Cap and Stem Surface Textures

12

IV. Tubes (pores)
a. Pattern (plate 9) —radiating or random.
b. Shape (plate 9)—angular or round, empty or stuffed.
c. Relation to stem (plate 7)—adnate, adnexed, decurrent, emarginate, free, seceding.

V. Stem (stipe)
a. Position (plate 9)—absent (sessile), central, eccentric, lateral.
b. Relation to cap—continuous (confluent) or separable from cap.
c. Shape (plate 10)—bulbous, clavate, equal, subbulbous.
d. Bulb (plate 10)—abrupt, abruptly bulbous, radicating, subradicating.
e. Surface texture (plate 6)—bare, costate, pubescent, punctate, reticulate, rugose, scabrous, striate.
f. Central portion (plate 10)—hollow, solid, stuffed, tubular.
g. Flesh (context) texture—cartilaginous, chalk-like, fibrillose, fibrous, sub-cartilaginous.

VI. Annulus (ring) see veils

VII. Volva (cup) see veils

VIII. Veils[1]
a. Universal veil (plate 11)—absent or present.
  1. Cap surface—calyptrate or patchy.
  2. Veil structure—membranous.
  3. Volva—banded (belts), crumbly, collared, floccose, free, marginate, saccate (cup-shaped), warty.
b. Partial veil (plate 11)—absent or present, on stem (annulus) or cap (appendiculate).
  1. Position on mushroom—appendiculate, inferior, medial, superior.

1. The remains of a universal veil at the base of the stem forms the volva. The remains of a partial veil on the upper portions of the stem forms the annulus.

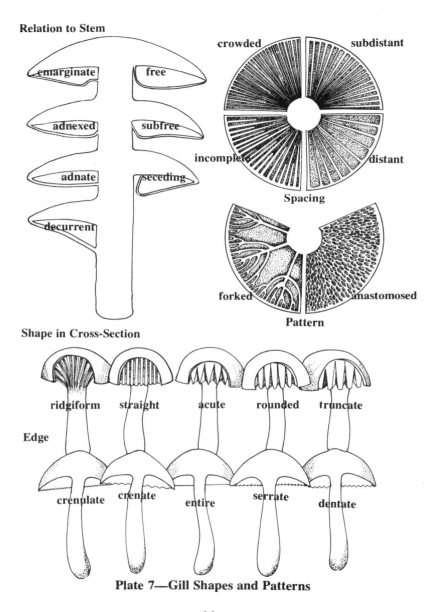

Relation to Stem

emarginate

free

adnexed

subfree

adnate

seceding

decurrent

crowded

subdistant

incomplete

distant

Spacing

forked

anastomosed

Pattern

Shape in Cross-Section

ridgiform   straight   acute   rounded   truncate

Edge

crenulate   crenate   entire   serrate   dentate

Plate 7—Gill Shapes and Patterns

14

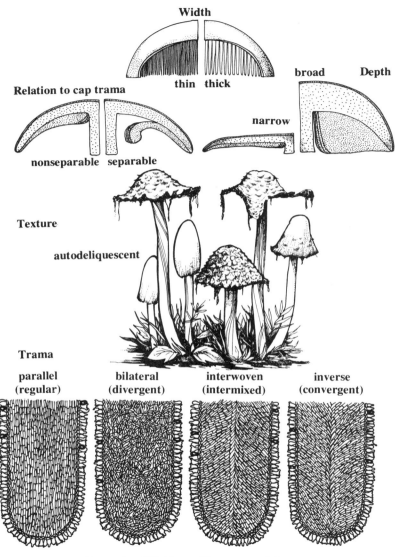

Width

thin thick

broad Depth

narrow

Relation to cap trama

nonseparable separable

Texture

autodeliquescent

Trama

parallel
(regular)

bilateral
(divergent)

interwoven
(intermixed)

inverse
(convergent)

Plate 8—Gill Sizes, Tramas and Textures

15

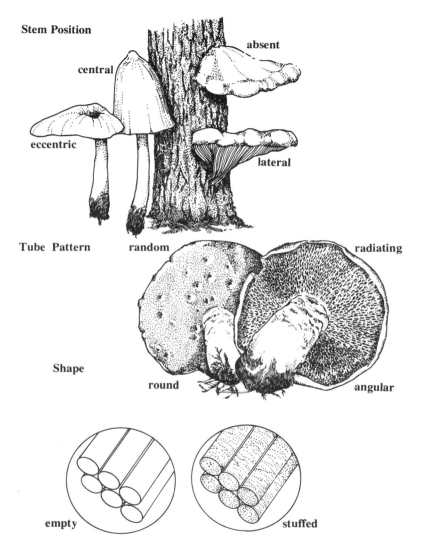

Stem Position

central

eccentric

absent

lateral

Tube Pattern   random   radiating

Shape

round   angular

empty   stuffed

Plate 9—Tube Patterns, Shapes and Positions

Stem Shape

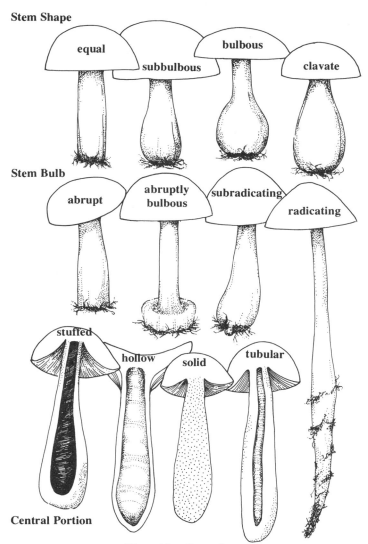

Stem Bulb

Central Portion

Plate 10—Stem Structures

17

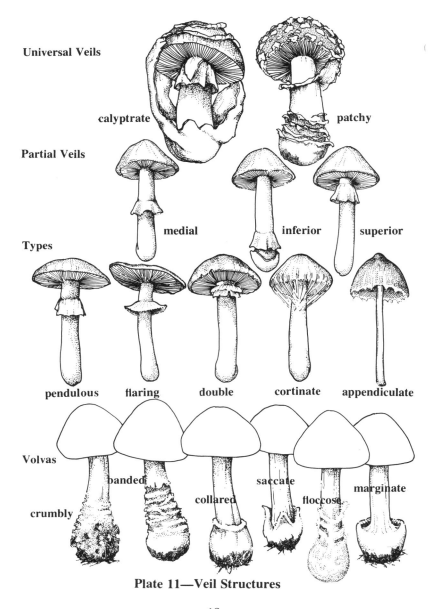

Universal Veils

calyptrate

patchy

Partial Veils

medial

inferior

superior

Types

pendulous   flaring   double   cortinate   appendiculate

Volvas

banded

saccate

marginate

collared

floccose

crumbly

Plate 11—Veil Structures

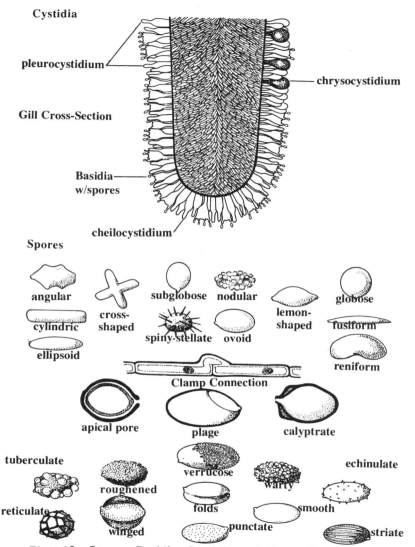

Cystidia

pleurocystidium

chrysocystidium

Gill Cross-Section

Basidia w/spores

cheilocystidium

Spores

angular

subglobose   nodular   globose

cross-shaped

cylindric

lemon-shaped   fusiform

spiny-stellate   ovoid

ellipsoid

reniform

Clamp Connection

apical pore   plage   calyptrate

tuberculate

verrucose   echinulate

roughened   warty

folds   smooth

reticulate

winged   punctate   striate

Plate 12—Spores, Basidia, Cystidia and Clamp Connections

19

    2. Type—double or single, evanescent, flaring, pendulous, persistent.

    3. Texture—cobwebby (cortinate), fibrillose, floccose, fragile, membranous.

IX. Spores.

  a. Shape (plate 12) –angular, cross-shaped, cylindric, ellipsoid, fusiform, globose, lemon-shaped, nodular, ovoid, reniform, spiny-stellate, subglobose.

  b. Ornamentation (plate 12) –echinulate, folds, punctate, reticulate, roughened, smooth, striate, tuberculate, verrucose, warty, winged.

  c. Apical pore(plate 12)–absent or present.

  d. Plage (plate 12)–absent or present.

  e. Calyptra(plate 12)–absent or present.

X. Cystidia (sterile hairs)—absent or present.

  a. Types—cheilocystidium, chrysocystidium, pleurocystidium.

XI. Basidia(plate 12)—four-spored, two-spored.

XII. Clamp connections(plate 12)—absent or present.

Microscopic Features

    Field identification of water buffalo, maple trees, or killer whales is easy because they abound in features which can be instantly recognized by your own senses. Animals and plants such as worms and mosses are simpler in form; hence they are more difficult to recognize in the field as a species distinct from another close relative.

    In the fungi, microscopic features are sometimes needed to identify a mushroom, or to place an unknown into a major group. It is indeed possible to recognize mushroom species primarily on the basis of microscopic features, but in this book we will use micro-scopic features as aids which will be used only as needed.

Spores should be measured in a mounting fluid such as 3% potassium hydroxide. Measurements from gill sections should be avoided since these spores are frequently immature. Ideally, spores from spore prints should be used. If you are in a rush, place a slide under the cap for just twenty to thirty minutes, or attempt to scrape some from spore deposits on the cap or stem. In order to measure spores and to determine the type and extent of ornament-ation, your microscope should be equipped with a good quality oil immersion (1000x) optical system. This means an investment of $600 or more. Plate 12 shows some of the various forms and modes of sculpturing which these spores have.

Spores are perhaps the easiest microscopic feature to de-monstrate. The remaining features require adeptness at freehand sectioning. Freehand sections may be taken quite easily with a razor. Take a 5 mm wedge of cap and gill. Squeeze the gills together between the thumb and forefinger. Now wet a **sharp** single edge razor blade and using the thumbnail as a guide, saw gently (in 10 micron units!). Cut thin sections like this ten to twenty times and wash onto a small dish of water. Pick out four to five nice sections and place them on a clean slide with potassium hydroxide (KOH). Drop on a cover slip, and you are ready to examine them.

Thin sections of gill wedges are essential in properly identify-ing many mushrooms. The bilateral gill tissue of the Amanitaceae is unique to this family, and hence is very useful in diagnosing *Amanita* poisoning. Basidia and cystidia, which line the gill sur-face, are also essential to view at times. Cystidia (plate 12), which line the face of the gills, are pleurocystidia, while those on the gill edges are cheilocystidia. These elusive structures are sometimes quite necessary to find. *Stropharia* is readily distinguished by chrysocystidia, which are visible as large encrusted structures filled with a golden fluid when mounted in potassium hydroxide.

21

The flesh of the mushroom, or cap trama, is sometimes studied to determine major groups, especially the Russulaceae. These mushrooms (*Russula* and *Lactarius*) have numerous spherical cells (sphaerocysts) which may be clustered among filamentous units. The cutis (skin) of the cap is either filamentous or cellular under the microscope. Again, freehand sections are frequently necessary to place an unknown in the proper group.

Some simple spot tests and colour reactions are commonly used as an additional identifying characteristic. A spot test notes the reaction of the mushroom to iodine, ferrous sulphate, ammonia, sulphovanilla, potassium hydroxide, etc. In this book, we have limited spot tests to Meltzer's reagent, which is an iodine solution of the following:

Potassium Iodide	1.5 gr
Iodine	0.5 gr
Water	20.0 gr
Chloral hydrate	22.0 gr
	44.0 gr

Meltzer's reagent is useful for demonstrating amyloid or dextrinoid features of spores or tissues. Amyloid spores show a typical starch or blue-black colour reaction in mass or singly. Dextrinoid spores are reddish when treated with Meltzer's reagent.

A useful reference for further information on the microscopic anatomy of mushrooms and their chemical features is *Agaricales in Modern Taxonomy* by Rolf Singer.

Mushroom Keys

If you are following the procedure outlined on page 7 you now have a pile of specimens, accurately described, along with their spore prints. Sort out those specimens which you hope to identify and faithfully compare your notes to both the key (page 24) and the mushroom descriptions in the text. The beginner should confidently approach a mushroom key with the knowledge that it was written for him.

How to Write and Use a Key

1. Using the specimens you have collected, sort out 5 of your best, most diverse specimens.
2. Prepare a list of macroscopic features for each specimen, following the descriptive terms from the previous section.
3. At this point it is time to learn about keys. You may have already noticed that identification of mushrooms is possible by matching written descriptions and pictures to your fungi. A better way to identify is possible—a key. Keys are aids to identification written by an expert who guides the eye of the student over the important features of the mushroom. Keys, therefore, are written for the student, not the expert.

In order to illustrate how a key works, we are going to show you how to write one yourself.

Rules

1. A key is like a roadway which has only two branched (dichotomous) intersections.
2. Each intersection (couplet) is actually a question which asks: is it A or is it not A?
3. Each question, whenever possible, refers to a trait which is not subjective (e.g., not large, small, thick, narrow), but instead a measurable feature.

Following is a key to distinguish between apples, bears, goats, potatoes, and frogs:

1. Reacts by moving when poked with a stick
   2. Horns present on head ....goat
   2. Horns not present on head
      3. With fur ....bear
      3. Without fur ....frog
1. May roll slightly when poked with stick, but no
   visible independent reaction
   4. Occurs beneath the ground ....potato
   4. Occurs on trees above ground ....apple

    Since we all know about these organisms, I'm sure you have your own ideas on how to write a similar key. Try it. After this key is completed, try writing another key to any 5 different mushrooms. Use your list of macroscopic features prepared earlier for a source of "distinctions."

Key To Genera With Poisonous Species

1. Lower surface of fruiting body variously arranged but lacking radiating plates (gills)
   2. Lower surface of fruiting body bearing hymenium (fertile layer)
      3. Lower surface a porose layer that easily separates from upper layer
         4. Fruiting body with non-scaly cap and stem, no veil, and amber-brown, olive - brown or yellow-brown spores ....*Boletus* (p. 83)
         4. Not as above ....other boletes
      3. Lower surface covered by rib-like folds
         5. Spores ochre ....*Gomphus* (p. 71)
         5. Spores not ochre ....other genera
   2. Upper surface of fruiting body bearing hymenium (fertile layer)
      6. Fruiting body branched, branches oriented upward with rounded or pointed tips; spores ochre coloured ....*Ramaria* (p. 92)

6. Fruiting body cup-shaped, disc-shaped or irregularly-shaped
    7. Fruiting body stalked; cap a cup folded back on stem
        8. Cap a series of pits and ridges attached only at stem apex ....*Verpa* (p. 86)
        8. Cap not as above
            9. Cap saddle-shaped ....*Helvella* (p. 90)
            9. Cap brain-like, convoluted
                10. Stem convoluted .....*Neogyromitra* (p. 87)
                10. Stem not convoluted ......*Gyromitra* (p. 89)
    7. Fruiting body sessile or nearly so
        11. Fruiting body originally globose, subterranean, later above ground and splitting stellately ....*Sarcosphaera* (p. 94)
        11. Fruiting body cup-shaped, spores elliptical, and asci bluing in iodine .....*Peziza* (p. 90)
1. Lower surface of fruiting body with radiating plates (gills)
    12. Spores black
        13. Gill surface mottled from uneven maturation of spores; colour of spores retained when dropped in concentrated sulphuric acid ....*Panaeolus* (p. 82)
        13. Gill surface evenly coloured; either gills dissolve into a black liquid or cap plicate-striate ....*Coprinus* (p. 80)
    12. Spores not black
        14. Spores dark
            15. Spores with purple overtones, filamentous cuticle
                16. Gills free, spores purple-brown to chocolate ....*Agaricus* (p. 56)
                16. Gills attached
                    17. Chrysocystidia present; cap usually brightly coloured ....*Naematoloma* (p. 79)

25

17. Chrysocystidia absent; cap
usually with brown tones ...... *Psilocybe* (p. 74)
15. Spores brown to yellow-brown, without
trace of purple or lilac
  18. Cuticle under hand lens cellular, not
fibrous; spore print rusty brown ... *Conocybe* (p. 71)
  18. Cuticle fibrous
    19. Gills decurrent and easily separ-
able from flesh of cap .... *Paxillus* (p. 56)
    19. Gills if decurrent not easily sep-
arable from flesh of cap
      20. Younger specimens with
definite cobwebby veil
        21. Gills adnate becoming
emarginate .... *Cortinarius* (p. 64)
        21. Gills adnexed to decur-
rent usually brightly-
coloured, stem usually
yellow .... *Gymnopilus* (p.73)
      20. Cortina absent, however
may have fibrillose veil
        22. Cap viscid .... *Hebeloma* (p. 59)
        22. Cap dry
          23. Surface covered
with mealy powder ... *Phaeolepiota*
(p. 69)
          23. Surface not as above
            24. Cap distinctly
fibrillose .... *Inocybe* (p. 67)
            24. Cap not fibril-
lose or faintly
so, gills white
edged under
hand lens ...... *Galerina* (p. 61)
14. Spores pale or pink
  25. Spores pink, gills sinuate .... *Rhodophyllus* (p. 52)
  25. Spores pale to white

26

26. Volva or annulus present
    27. Volva present, annulus may be
        present . . . .*Amanita* (p. 46)
    27. Volva absent, annulus present,
        gills free . . . . *Lepiota* (p. 44)
26. Volva and annulus absent
    28. Chalklike consistency to stem
        29. Milk-like material exudes
            from flesh or gills when cut .*Lactarius* (p. 41)
        29. Milk-like material absent,
            flesh very fragile . . . .*Russula* (p. 40)
    28. Fibrous consistency to stem
        30. Gills luminescent . . . .*Omphalotus*
                               (p. 38)
        30. Gills not luminescent
            31. Gills sinuate . . . .*Tricholoma*
                               (p. 28)
            31. Gills adnate, adnexed or
                decurrent
                32. Gills thick, waxy . . . . .*Hygrophorus*
                               (p. 31)
                32. Not as above
                    33. Cap bell-shaped
                        to campanulate . . .*Mycena* (p. 33)
                    33. Not as above
                        34. Cap umbili-
                            cate to
                            infundibuli-
                            form . . . .*Clitocybe* (p. 34)
                      34. Cap convex
                        to plane . . . .*Lyophyllum*
                                        (p. 37)

Genera Descriptions

The format used in this book is slightly different than in most mushroom books. A general description is given of the genus in which one or more poisonous species exist. This covers the basic parts of the mushroom, including the shape of the fruiting body, cap, gills, stem, flesh, cuticle, annulus, volva, spores and gill trama. Wherever necessary for definite identification microscopic characters are also included. Among the microscopic features that you can observe are gill trama, spore shape, cheilocystidia, caulocystidia, pleurocystidia, chrysocystidia, basidia and clamp connections. For help in identifying these features, refer to the section on how to demonstrate microscopic features of mushrooms on page 20. Following the genus description is a passage which describes the features which typify this genus and a comparison of it to related genera.

A final major passage names and describes all of the poisonous species in the genus and compares them to the non-poisonous species.

Tricholoma   Colour Plate I

Description—*Fruiting Body:* tricholomoid; *Cap:* convex to plane; *Cuticle:* a dense layer of filamentous hyphae, interwoven, parallel or subparallel; *Flesh:* thick; *Gills:* usually emarginate, sinuate, or occasionally adnexed, thin to medium broad; *Stem:* central, fleshy to fleshy fibrillose, thick, confluent with cap, lacking volva or annulus; *Spores:* white, ellipsoid to subglobose, rarely cross shaped, smooth, nonamyloid; *Gill Trama:* parallel to somewhat interwoven; usually terrestrial.

Distinguishing Features—1) white spores; 2) tricholomoid habit; 3) emarginate-sinuate gills; and 4) terrestrial habit.

28

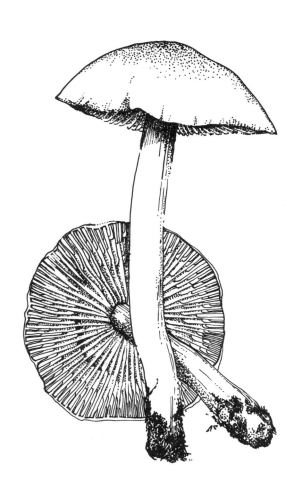

Tricholoma sulphureum (75% actual size)

Remarks—A number of genera have at least some species which can be mistaken for *Tricholoma*. Of these, *Clitocybe spp.* differs in having decurrent gills, *Oudemansiella* has a hymeniform or palisade-like cuticle, *Tricholomopsis* has cheilocystidia and a cap usually overlaid with dense fibrils, and *Leucopaxillus* and *Melanoleuca* both have amyloid spores. *Leucopaxillus* also has an opaque look, while *Melanoleuca* has a cartilaginous, rather than fleshy, stem. Lastly, *Hygrophorus* generally differs in being a smaller mushroom with a conic cap. However, a few species of *Hygrophorus* do closely resemble *Tricholoma*. Macroscopically, they differ in having widely-spaced, thick, waxy gills. Microscopically, their basidia are typically more than six times the length of the spores.

Name Derivation—In Greek, tricho means a hair or a fringe, and loma is a border or margin.

Poisonous Species—*Tricholoma* species can be divided into groups according to the following key.

1. Clamp connections absent or present only on
   basidia base, or stem covering, or scattered in carpophore
   2. Cuticle of cap interwoven . . . . .Group 2
   2. Cuticle of cap subparallel with a subtomentose
      to squamose appearance . . . . .Group 4
1. Clamp connections present in all hyphae
   3. Cuticle of cap interwoven . . . . .Group 1
   3. Cuticle of cap subparallel . . . . .Group 3

Group 1 has a single reportedly poisonous species, *T. saponaceum*. This species, although quite variable, does not resemble any other. The cap is greenish-gray, has smooth scales, and a soapy taste and smell. The stem surface is white, flushed with the cap colour, while the flesh in the base of the stem is pink.

Group 2 has two poisonous species, *T. sulphureum* and *T.*

album. *T. sulphureum* is quite easily distinguished by its yellow stem, gills and cap, and the strong odour of coal gas. One other species, *T. inamoenum*, has this odour, but it is white to pale ivory in colour. *T. chrysenteroides* also resembles *T. sulphureum*, but is lighter yellow and lacks the odour. *T. album* has a glabrous, moist, white cap and solid stem. Of the other white species, *T. terriferum* and *T. resplendens* have a viscid cap, *T. columbetta* and *T. fumescens* are minutely tomentose, *T. grande* is squamulose, *T. leucocephalum* has a hollow stem, *T. unifactum* grows in clusters, and *T. acerbum* has a cap margin with radiating ridges.

Group 3 has a single poisonous species, *T. pardinum*. It is the only species of this group and is identified by the white dry cap with gray scales, white gills and white stem. It could be mistaken for other white species as outlined in Group 2.

Group 4 also has a single poisonous species, *T. virgatum*. It has a dry, silky, white umbonate cap streaked with gray to black fibrils. The gray colour and prominent acute umbo separate it from other species.

Where and When—*Tricholoma species* typically occur late summer to fall in mixed woods. However, *T. columbetta* usually appears in beech or birch woods, *T. leucocephalum* under conifers, *T. resplendens* under hardwoods, and *T. unifactum* under hemlock.

Nature of Toxin—Type III, gastrointestinal, symptoms mild to severe. One species, *T. pardinum*, is usually very severe.

Hygrophorus   Colour Plate II

Description—*Fruiting Body:* tricholomoid; *Cap:* fleshy, often viscid to glutinous; *Cuticle:* of radiately arranged filamentous hyphae; *Gills:* thick and waxy, adnate to deeply decurrent; *Stem:* subcartilaginous to fleshy; *Spores:* white, smooth, nonamyloid; *Basidia:* usually more than six times the spore length;

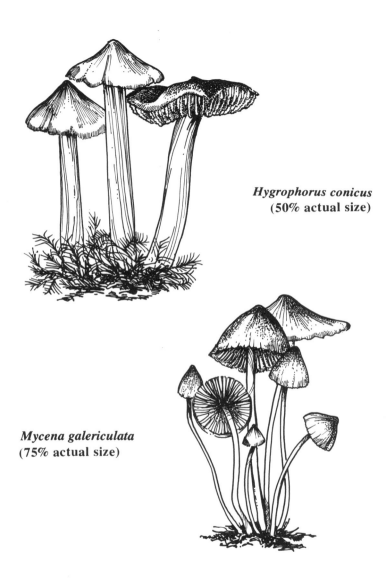

Hygrophorus conicus
(50% actual size)

Mycena galericulata
(75% actual size)

32

Gill Trama: Bilateral, or interwoven; *Cystidia:* rare; *Pleurocystidia:* absent.

Distinguishing Features—1) thick waxy gills; 2) white smooth spores; 3) fleshy stem; and 4) elongate basidia.

Remarks—This genus is easily confused with several other white-spored genera. *Laccaria*, which can appear to have waxy gills, differs in having echinulate spores. *Armillaria, Tricholoma* and *Clitocybe* are also likely to be confused with *Hygrophorus*. None of these, however, have thick waxy gills. In addition, *Tricholoma* differs in having basidia less than six times the spore length, and *Armillaria* has an annulus.

Name Derivation—*Hygrophorus* is from the Greek hygroph for moist and orus for to bear.

Poisonous Species—One species, *H. conicus*, may be poisonous. It is distinguished by a bright orange, conic cap; white to yellow subfree gills; and a long, orange, thick, hollow stem with a white base. The entire mushroom stains black upon bruising. Only one other species, *H. nigrescens,* blackens, and it has not been reported from North America.

Where and When—*H. conicus* grows in woods, fields, and bogs, from spring through fall.

Nature of Toxin—Type III, gastrointestinal.

Mycena Colour Plate III

Description—*Fruiting Body:* mycenoid; *Cap:* conic to campanulate, thin, translucent, striate, fleshy to membranous; *Cuticle:* with epicutis of filamentous hyphae and subcutis of inflated cells; *Flesh:* thin; *Gills:* usually ascending adnate but more rarely adnexed, sinuate or decurrent; *Stem:* thin, cartilaginous, tubular or hollow, glabrous or appressed fibrillose, lacking annulus or volva; *Spores:* white, subglobose, ovoid, ellipsoid, or cylindric, smooth or nodular, amyloid or nonamyloid; *Gill Trama:* regular to interwoven; *Cheilocystidia and Pleurocystidia:* usually present.

Distinguishing Features—1) white spores; 2) mycenoid habit; 3) small size and fragile appearance; 4) bell-shaped to campanulate cap; and 5) two-layered cuticle.

Remarks—This genus can be separated from most others by its white spores, lack of annulus and volva, and small fragile size. Two genera, *Marasmius* and *Collybia*, could be confused with it. *Marasmius* has a tough stalk which tends to revive when moistened. *Collybia* tends to be larger in size, convex to plane in shape with the margin of the cap incurved at first. Neither of these has a cap subcutis.

Name Derivation—*Mycena* in Greek is a fungus.

Poisonous Species—We have not been able to ascertain which species are supposedly poisonous, so members of this genus should be avoided as a precaution. Because of their small size, they are hardly worthy of pot-hunting efforts.

Where and When—*Mycena species* are found in lawns, pastures and woods from early spring through late fall.

Nature of Toxin—Type III, gastrointestinal.

Clitocybe Colour Plate IV

Description—*Fruiting Body:* clitocyboid; *Cap:* umbilicate or infundibuliform, often depressed with margin incurved at first; *Epicutis:* interwoven filamentous hyphae; *Flesh:* thin, soft; *Gills:* decurrent or adnate-decurrent, close, narrow, white or concolourous with cap; *Stem:* central, fibrous fleshy, lacking annulus or volva; *Spores:* white, greenish or pinkish buff, globose, ovoid, ellipsoid, nonamyloid, smooth or roughened.

Distinguishing Features—1) white spores; 2) umbilicate, infundibuliform or depressed cap; 3) decurrent gills; and 4) fleshy stem.

Remarks—*Clitocybe* is a fairly distinct genus with white spores and decurrent gills, but lacking an annulus and volva. *Marasmius, Hygrophorus, Mycena* and *Collybia* all have species which resemble it. None of these, except *Hygrophorus*, typically have both strongly decurrent gills and an umbilicate or infundibuliform cap. *Hygrophorus*, however, has distinct waxy gills. Three other white-spored genera could also be confused with *Clitocybe*. *Leucopaxillus,* a genus with decurrent gills, differs in having amyloid spores, while *Lyophyllum* has dark granules in the basidia when stained with acetocarmine. The last genus, *Omphalina*, looks like a small *Clitocybe*. It seldom, however, grows over 4 cm tall, and lacks the fleshy stem of *Clitocybe*.

Name Derivation—*Clitocybe* is Greek for sloping head.

Poisonous Species—*Clitocybe* is a very large genus, containing many species which cannot be identified without a microscope. All known poisonous species are in section Candecantes, which is characterized by 1) a white, buff, yellow or pink cap that is initially convex but becomes either quickly depressed or depressed in age; 2) a central, fibrous to fibrous-fleshy stem; 3) white, buff, yellow, or pink gills; 4) white, ellipsoid to ovoid spores containing a globose oil drop; and 5) clamp connections. All of these features must be demonstrated to place a mushroom in this group.

Three poisonous species are known. These are *C. cerussata* var. *difformis, C. dealbata*, and *C. rivulosa*. All of these have a moist but not hygrophanous cap smaller than 8 cm in diameter, and a terrestrial growth habit.

C. cerussata var. *difformis* is easily identified in the field. It has a shiny white plicate to irregularly lobed cap, solid stem, and grows in dense masses.

C. dealbata has a white disc-shaped cap with a wavy margin, stuffed, mealy to pruinose stem, and usually grows in twos or fairy rings. It may be confused with *C. candicans,* which, however, has a glabrous hollow stem, *C. albissima*, which also grows in fairy rings but has a very dry cap, or *Marasmius oreades*, the fairy ring

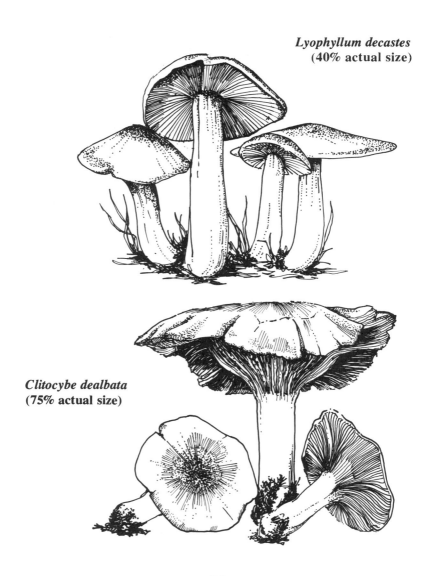

Lyophyllum decastes
(40% actual size)

Clitocybe dealbata
(75% actual size)

mushroom, which is pale brown and revives when moistened.

C. *rivulosa* has a pink to brown concentrically furrowed cap. The stem is white to pink and often curved. This one resembles *C. dealbata* closely except for colour, and could be confused with the same mushrooms as mentioned for that species.

Where and When—All of the *Clitocybe* species except *C. dealbata* most commonly occur on leafy ground in the woods during the fall. *C. dealbata* is found in the open in pastures, lawns or open woods.

Nature of Toxin—Type II B, muscarine. This toxin has given *C. dealbata* the common name of the sweat-producing *Clitocybe*.

Lyophyllum   Colour Plate V

Description—*Fruiting Body:* clitocyboid; *Cap:* glabrous to hygrophanous, white, gray, black or brown, dry, fleshy; *Cuticle:* not differentiated; *Flesh:* thick, often staining yellow, yellow-gray, or black when bruised; *Gills:* white to sordid, attached, adnate to decurrent; *Stem:* central without annulus or volva; *Spores:* white, nonamyloid, usually smooth, globose, ovoid, ellipsoid, cylindric, fusiform, or angular; *Basidia:* with numerous carminophilous granules.

Distinguishing Features—1) carminophilous granules in basidia; 2) white spores; and 3) a grayish-tan soapy look to the gills and cap.

Remarks—*Lyophyllum* is a genus intermittent between *Tricholoma* and *Clitocybe*. *Tricholoma* is delineated fairly well by its sinuate-emarginate gills, while *Clitocybe* is a smaller, less fleshy mushroom with more strongly decurrent gills. Both lack the grayish-tan soapy look of *Lyophyllum*.

Name Derivation—Lyo means free and phyllum means leaves or gills.

Poisonous Species—*Lyophyllum decastes*, a common poisonous species, has a cream to tan smooth cap and whitish gills and stem. It differs from *Lyophyllum multiceps*, (frequently reported edible) mainly in its solitary growth habit. *L. multiceps* grows in dense clusters, sometimes consisting of hundreds of mushrooms. Recent studies however, have cast some doubt on the separation of these two species. We must now consider both species poisonous since the specimen illustrated in this text was given to two friends. Both unfortunate people came down with violent gastrointestinal attacks.

Where and When—*Lyophyllum decastes* and *L. multiceps* are both found in the fall, after the rains start, in grassy areas and along roadsides.

Nature of Toxin—Type III, gastrointestinal.

Omphalotus

Description—*Fruiting Body:* pleurotoid to clitocyboid in habit, fleshy; *Cap:* non-hygrophanous; *Epicutis:* little differentiated; *Gills:* luminescent, brightly coloured, decurrent; *Stem:* fibrous or fleshy, central or eccentric; *Spores:* white, smooth, subglobose to short ellipsoid, nonamyloid; *Gill Trama:* regular to irregular; *Clamp Connections:* present; *Habitat:* lignicolous.

Distinguishing Features—1) luminescent gills; and 2) white spores.

Remarks—This genus is composed of the species with luminescent gills which were originally in *Pleurotus* and *Clitocybe*. It differs from *Lampteromyces*, which also has luminescent gills, by the absence of a veil. In addition, *Pleurotus* has 1) cylindric, not pure white spores; 2) more irregular gill trama (almost intermixed); 3) more eccentric stem; and 4) distinct subhymenium. *Armillariella* lacks clamp connections, and *Clitocybe* has spores with rough walls if they are white and lacks bright colours.

Name Derivation—Ompha is from the Greek, meaning umbilicus, and otus means ear.

Poisonous Species—*Omphalotus* has one species *O. olearius* which is poisonous. This species has a convex to plane, yellow to

38

Russula emetica
(75% actual size)

Omphalotus olearius
(50% actual size)

orange-yellow cap with an inrolled margin. The gills and stem are concolourous with the cap. It may be confused with *Cantharellus cibarius*, which is identical in colour but has ridges instead of plate-like gills.

Where and When—*O. olearius* grows on stumps or decaying wood in fall.

Nature of Toxin—Type III, gastrointestinal.

Russula Colour Plate VI

Description—*Fruiting Body:* stipitate-pileate; *Cap:* fleshy, broadly convex to plane or depressed with elevated margin; *Flesh:* fragile due to nests of sphaerocysts among connective tissue, without latex; *Gills:* free or attached; *Stem:* thick, chalklike, without volva and annulus; *Spores:* white, cream, yellow, pinkish or orange, amyloid, reticulate or verrucose.

Distinguishing Features—1) fragile flesh and chalklike stem; and 2) lack of latex.

Remarks—The only genus that closely resembles *Russula* is *Lactarius*. These mushrooms exude a latex when cut or broken. No other genera have a chalklike stem lacking fibrous elements. When in doubt, there is a *Russula* test. Throw the mushroom at a tree. If it shatters, it's *Russula*. Perhaps this is the best thing to do, since they are nearly impossible to identify as to species.

Name Derivation—*Russula* means reddish.

Poisonous Species—One species of *Russula, R. emetica,* is considered poisonous. It has a bright red cap, pure white gills and stem, and an intense peppery taste. There are many closely related species with white stem and gills, but their caps are shades of pink, salmon or yellow. One species, *R. rosacea*, is often mistaken for *R. emetica*. However, it has a rose or red stem and yellow gills.

Where and When—*Russula species* appear when rains occur in spring, summer, or fall. *R. rosacea* and *R. emetica* usually occur

40

under conifers, especially Douglas fir.
Nature of Toxin—Type III, gastrointestinal. *R. emetica* derives its name from the severe vomiting it causes.

Lactarius   Colour Plates VII-VIII

Description—*Fruiting Body:* stipitate-pileate; *Cap:* fleshy; *Flesh:* fragile, containing sphaerocysts among connective tissue, exuding a milky latex when cut; *Gills:* subdecurrent to decurrent, wedge-shaped; *Stem:* chalklike, central, without annulus or volva; *Spores:* white, cream, yellow, pinkish, or orange, amyloid.
Distinguishing Features—1) latex.
Remarks—No other genus has this milk. *Russula* resembles *Lactarius* in general appearance and fragile context, but lacks the latex.
Name Derivation—*Lactarius* means giving lac or milk.
Poisonous Species—*Lactarius* is another large genus. It is easily divided into three natural groups: 1) milk white, unchanging; 2) milk white, changing colour when exposed to air; and 3) milk initially coloured other than white.

In Group 1 are eight species which are either poisonous or suspected of being so. Two of these species, *L. torminosus* and *L. trivialis*, have a viscid cap, at least when moist. *L. torminosus* is further identified by the flesh-coloured zonate cap and hairy cap margin. Do not confuse this with *L. insulsus*, which is copper-orange and lacks the hairs. *L. trivialis* has a non-zonate smoky-gray cap which is often tinted purple, an acrid taste, yellow spores, and green-staining flesh or gills. This mushroom closely resembles *L. affinis*, which has a pale yellow cap, *L. vietus*, which is lilac-gray but has flesh that stains gray, and *L. mucidus*, which has white spores, is putty-coloured, and has a very glutinous cap and stem.

Four of the species in Group 1 have a tomentose cap. These are *L. vellereus, L. helvus, L. lignyotus,* and *L. fuliginosus. L.*

vellereus is white and is tomentose on both the disc and margin. This separates it from *L. deceptivus*, which is woolly on the margin only. It also resembles *L. subvellereus*, which, however, stains green; *L. piperatus*, which has crowded, repeatedly forked gills; and *L. pergamenus*, which has a very wrinkled cap. Be sure to look for latex, as it also resembles *R. brevipes*. *L. helvus* has a light tawny cap and grows in swamps. Two closely related species, *L. corrugis* and *L. hygrophoroides*, grow in woods. *L. lignyotus* is a velvety sooty brown, and *L. fuliginosus* is a smooth gray-brown. Both are readily identified as they turn red when bruised.

The last two poisonous members of this group, *L. rufus* and *L. pyrogalus*, have a glabrous cap. *L. pyrogalus* has a zonate gray cap, yellow gills, and flesh that bruises red. *L. rufus* is bay red to reddish-brown and tastes acrid. It resembles two orange-brown species, *L. hygrophoroides* and *L. camphoratus*, which have a mild taste.

Group 2 has four poisonous members. *L. uvidus* is easily distinguished, as it has latex which is initially white but stains the flesh or gills purple on exposure to air. *L. lignyotus* and *L. fuliginosus* have latex which is initially white but turns pink. *L. lignyotus* is velvety and sooty brown, while *L. fuliginosus* is smooth and gray-brown. No other species resemble these three. *L. scrobiculatus* has latex which is initially white but becomes yellow. It is distinguished from *L. cilicioides*, which has a woolly cap, by having hairs only on the cap margin.

Group 3 has no poisonous species.

Where and When—All *Lactarius species* mentioned appear in summer or fall whenever the rains come. *L. affinis*, *L. torminosus*, *L. trivialis*, *L. vellereus*, *L. pergamenus*, *L. piperatus*, and *L. pyrogalus* appear in mixed woods. *L. cilicioides* grows on sandy soil under pine, while *L. fuliginosus* and *L. vietus* are usually found in oak, maple, or beech woods. *L. mucidus*, *L. rufus*, *L. lignyotus*, and *L. scrobiculatus* grow under conifers often in mossy, swampy ground, while *L. helvus*, *L. deceptivus*, *L. uvidus*, and *L. cam-*

Lactarius scrobiculatus
(75% actual size)

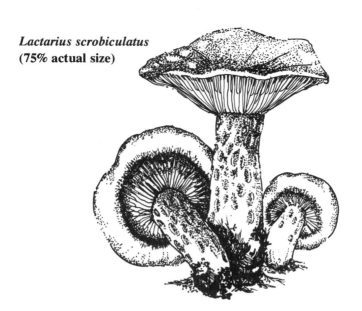

Lactarius vellereus
(50% actual size)

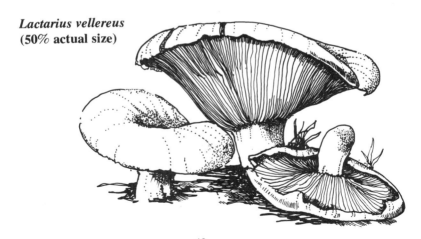

phoratus grow in mixed woods on mossy, swampy ground. *L. hygrophoroides* and *L. insulsus* are found in deciduous woods.

Nature of Toxin—Type III, gastrointestinal; the toxin is particularly severe in *L. torminosus* and in uncooked specimens of other species.

Lepiota

Description—*Fruiting Body:* stipitate-pileate, fleshy; *Cap:* silky to fibrillose or with patch-like scales; *Flesh:* soft; *Epicutis:* of appressed narrow hyphae or a palisade of differentiated cells often breaking down into scales; *Gills:* free; *Stem:* central, with annulus, no volva; *Annulus:* persistent or evanescent; *Spores:* white, cream, or greenish, of diverse shapes, smooth, amyloid or nonamyloid; *Gill Trama:* parallel or interwoven.

Distinguishing Features—1) white spores; 2) free gills; 3) annulus; and 4) no volva.

Remarks—White-spored species resembling *Lepiota* are *Cystoderma, Armillaria, Oudemansiella, Amanita* and *Limacella.* The first three of these have attached gills. *Amanita* always has a volva and *Limacella* has the remains of a universal veil which appears as glutinous or viscid spots on the cap when it is fresh.

Chamaeota and *Agaricus* both resemble *Lepiota* in having an annulus and free gills. However, *Chamaeota* has pink spores and *Agaricus* has chocolate to purple-brown spores.

Name Derivation—Lepi is Greek for a scale and ota is ear.

Poisonous Species—One species of *Lepiota* is considered poisonous, *L. helveola*. It has a palisade-type cuticle, well-developed annulus, non-fusoid white spores, and is quite small. One other species generally considered a *Lepiota*, but now residing in the genus *Chlorophyllum*, is poisonous. This is *C. molybdites*. (A synonym of this is *L. morgani*.)

44

Lepiota helveola
(**100% actual size**)

Chlorophyllum molybdites
(***Lepiota morgani***)
(**35% actual size**)

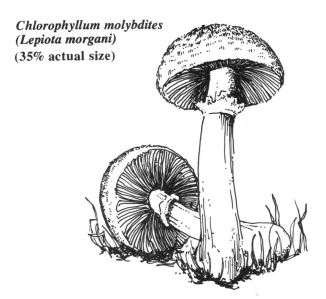

Chlorophyllum has green spores as opposed to the white ones of *Lepiota*. The cap is pink and scaly and the gills are white turning green. This is the only common species in this genus.

Where and When—*C. molybdites* often forms fairy rings in open woods or grassy areas in the fall.

Nature of Toxin—Type III, gastrointestinal (*C. molybdites*), type Ia, protoplasmic (*L. helveola*).

Amanita   Colour Plates IX-XII

Description—*Fruiting Body:* stipitate-pileate; *Cap:* ovoid when young and convex to nearly plane when mature; *Cuticle:* often with warts or patches from universal veil; *Flesh:* firm; *Gills:* free or nearly so, alternating with incomplete gills, white to yellow or grayish; *Stem:* central, easily separable from cap, with volva, usually with annulus, base often enlarged; *Spores:* white, cream, greenish, or rarely pink, smooth, globose, ovoid, ellipsoid, or subcylindric, amyloid or not; *Gill Trama:* bilateral.

Distinguishing Features—1) white spores; 2) free gills; 3) annulus; 4) volva; and 5) bilateral gill trama.

Remarks—No other white-spored species has a volva. However, *Lepiota* and *Limacella* have free gills and an annulus and could be confused with *Amanita*. One pink-spored species, *Volvariella*, does have a volva but can be separated by the spore colour.

Name Derivation—*Amanita* is a name given to some fungi by Galen, perhaps from Mt. Amanus.

Poisonous Species—The genus *Amanita* contains more poisonous species than any other genera—at least twenty and perhaps more. Due to the large number of species, these will be treated in nine groups of related species after the manner of Singer[1].

1. R. Singer, *Agaricales in Modern Taxonomy*, 2d ed., rev., (Weinheim: J. Cramer, 1962).

46

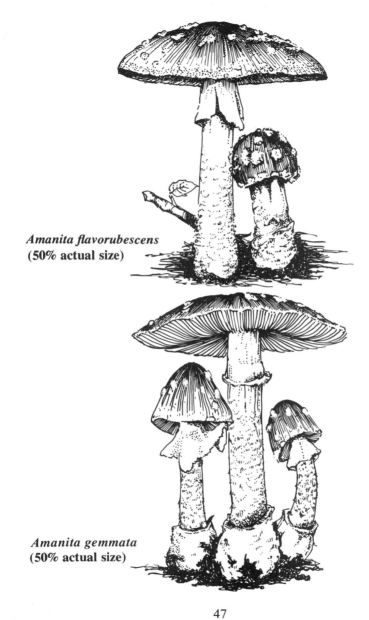

Amanita flavorubescens
(50% actual size)

Amanita gemmata
(50% actual size)

Key to groups of *Amanita*
1. Spores nonamyloid
  2. Spores globose to subglobose, annulus fragile,
    often disappearing
      3. Volva reduced to belts, bands, or warts ....Group 1
      3. Volva saccate, free, marginate, or crumbly,
        annulus absent ....Group 2
  2. Spores ellipsoid to cylindric
      4. Annulus and volva well-developed ....Group 3
      4. Annulus absent ....Group 4
1. Spores amyloid
  5. Volva cup-shaped to saccate, well-developed ....Group 5
  5. Volva little developed or in bands or crumbly
      6. Cap and stem covered with crumbly
        remains of volva ....Group 6
      6. Volva not crumbly
        7. Cap whitish; volva in belts ....Group 7
        7. Cap coloured; volva at base of stem,
          little developed ....Group 8

Group 1 is characterized by a fragile annulus which may disappear, a volva reduced to belts, bands, or warts on the cap and subglobose spores. All five of the common species, *A. frostiana, A. gemmata, A. muscaria, A. pantherina* and *A. cothurnata* are either poisonous or suspected of being poisonous. These species can be told apart on field characters, but they do tend to integrate. *A. cothurnata* has a white cap with a yellow tinge on the disc. All of the rest are coloured. *A. gemmata* has a pale yellow cap with white to brown warts and a free marginal collar around the apex of the bulb. It integrates with *A. pantherina*, which is smoky-brown to yellow. *A. gemmata* has a fragile membranous annulus which often disappears or is attached to the margin of the cap. *A. pantherina* has a floccose-membranous annulus with a yellow or brown margin.

A. muscaria varies in colour from white to bright yellow to brownish to deep red. It has white patches of veil on the cap. It is generally quite large, has a ragged volva present as rings or scales on the stem and broadly ellipsoid spores. Typically, *A. muscaria* refers to var. *muscaria*, the large red to orange variety of this mushroom. Three other varieties are also found which are mainly distinguished by cap colour. *A. muscaria* var. *alba* has a white cap, var. *umbrina* a brown cap, and var. *formosa* a yellow cap. *A. muscaria* var. *umbrina* has the habitat and shape of *A. muscaria* and the colour of *A. pantherina*. *A. muscaria* var. *formosa* is, in addition, broken down into three forms, a lemon yellow one, a light yellow one with a short stem, and a yellow one having brown over the disc. The last species in this group, *A. frostiana,* differs from *A. muscaria* only in its smaller size, globose spores, and a small boot-like volva.

Group 2 has no poisonous species. Species in this group lack an annulus, but have a well-developed volva and globose spores.

Group 3 is characterized by having both a well-developed annulus and volva. This group has two common species, one poisonous and one edible. The poisonous one, *A. spreta*, is pale brown to amber, occasionally with white patches on the cap. *A. caesarea*, the edible species, is bright orange.

Group 4 is identical to Group 2, except that the spores are ellipsoid. None of its species is known to be poisonous.

Group 5 contains seven species that have been reported as poisonous. These species resemble each other only to the extent that the spores are amyloid and the volva well developed.

Two species, *A. bisporigera* and *A. verna* are pure white. *A. bisporigera* differs from *A. verna* in having two spores on each basidium instead of four. *A. virosa* reported by Singer as a synonym of *A. verna* may actually be a separate species as it apparently does not stain yellow with KOH while *A. verna* and *A. bisporigera* do. One other white *Amanita, A. ocreata*, has been reported in California as poisonous. The whole group of white

Amanitas should be avoided.

Another poisonous species, *A. agglutinata*, has a white to brownish cap covered with white scales, a large brown membranous volva and no annulus.

The remaining four poisonous species in this group tend to blend together. *A. phalloides*, by far the most toxic, has a light yellow to greenish brown cap, a lighter stem varying from white to greenish yellow and a membranous volva with a jagged edge around a basal bulb. The annulus is well formed and superior. *A. brunnescens* has a brownish gray cap with a few warts and a fragile longitudinally split volva forming a shallow cup. It stains brown on the stem if it is bruised. *A. porphyria* has a grey brown cap, annulus, lower stem, and bulb. The last species, *A. citrina*, has a cap colour close to *A. phalloides* being yellow with a greenish tinge. The volva adheres to the bulb but the margin is distinct and free. This mushroom may in fact be edible as it was apparently served to the Mycological Society of France at a banquet in 1925 with no ill effects. It should be avoided due to the resemblance to *A. phalloides*.

Group 6 is characterized by a crumbly volva which leaves fragments on the cap, stem and annulus. The annulus is also crumbly, the cap white or coloured, and the spores ellipsoid to cylindric.

One species, *A. chlorinosma*, is considered poisonous. A second, *A. cinereoconia*, may be a small variety of the first. The cap is white with soft spines or dense floccose warts in the centre. The volva is floccose and the annulus fragile. The species is most definitely distinguished by the odour of chlorine.

Group 7 species have a white cap with pyramidal warts, a basal volva with warts, and ellipsoid to cylindric spores. This group has no proven poisonous species.

Group 8 species have a pigmented cap with warts, ellipsoid

spores, a little developed volva, and flesh that does not redden when exposed to air. This group has four common poisonous species and one non-poisonous one. These species tend to integrate with each other. *A. flavoconia* is bright yellow to orange, non-striate, with pale to yellow warts. The volva is yellow and granular powdery, and there are granular patches on the cap and stem. *A. flavorubescens* is very similar to *A. flavoconia*. It tends to be more light yellow to deep or olive yellow. The volva is membranous and tightly appressed to the bulb and stains reddish when bruised. The non-poisonous species, *A. rubescens*, may look like *A. flavorubescens*, although the cap is usually reddish-brown with floccose pink or gray scales. Both annulus and volva are fragile. The entire mushroom may stain reddish if bruised. *A. rubescens* is often confused with the browner *A. brunnescens* (Group 5), which stains reddish-brown and has globose spores and a marginal bulb.

The other two poisonous species in this group are brownish-gray. *A. excelsa*, however, has whitish-gray warts, concentric scales on the lower stem, and a marginate bulb, while *A. spissa* has grayish scales, a white pendulous annulus, and a gray volva.

Where and When—Many of the *Amanita species* can occur in several habitats over most of the year. *A. muscaria*, for example, can occur spring through fall in mixed woods, conifers, hardwoods or fields. Four species, *A. caesarea*, *A. excelsa*, *A. phalloides* and *A. spissa* occur mainly under oaks in summer and fall. Species occurring chiefly under conifers are *A. porphyria* (fall), *A. pantherina* (summer, fall, winter), *A. verna* (spring, summer, fall), and *A. gemmata* (fall). All of the other *Amanita species* listed occur in mixed woods summer through fall.

Nature of Toxin—

Type Ia, Cyclopeptide toxins present.

    A. bisporigera

    A. phalloides

    A. verna

Type IIa, Toggle Switch intoxication, ibotenic acid, and muscimole

    A. muscaria
    A. pantherina

Type III, Gastrointestinal

    A. cothurnata

Type IId[2], bufotenine

    A. citrina
    A. porphyria

Toxicity suspect, requires investigation

    A. agglutinata
    A. brunnescens
    A. chlorinosma
    A. excelsa
    A. flavoconia
    A. flavorubescens
    A. frostiana
    A. gemmata
    A. spissa
    A. ocreata

Rhodophyllus Colour Plate XIII

Description—*Fruiting Body:* stipitate-pileate; *Cap:* fleshy to membranous, convex to plane, margin incurved when young; *Gills:* attached, usually sinuate; *Stem:* central, fleshy to fleshy-fibrous, without annulus or volva, confluent with cap; *Spores:* pink to pinkish-brown, angular in frontal view and profile, smooth, nonamyloid.

2. It is not treated in this book because it is toxic only when injected.

Distinguishing Features—1) attached gills; 2) fleshy central stem; and 3) pink angular spores.

Remarks—There has been much dissension in separating the pink-spored Agarics into distinct genera. A few species with nonangular pale pink spores are placed in the white- or pale-spored genera, *Collybia, Lepiota, Clitocybe, Russula, Lactarius,* and *Amanita.* The more closely related genera, *Volvariella, Chamaeota, Pluteus, Claudopus, Clitopilus, Leptonia,* and *Nolanea,* have distinctly pink to pinkish-brown spores. *Volvariella, Pluteus,* and *Chamaeota,* however, have free gills, non-angular spores, and an inverse trama. In addition, *Volvariella* has a volva and *Chamaeota* an annulus. *Claudopus* has an eccentric or lateral stem, while *Leptonia* and *Nolanea* have slender stems and thin caps that are umbilicate, conic, or campanulate. *Clitopilus* is perhaps the closest to *Rhodophyllus.* Its spores are not angular in both profile and end view, and its gills are decurrent to broadly adnate.

Name Derivation—*Rhodophyllus* is from red and leaf or plant.

Poisonous Species—Since this is a large genus, non-poisonous species are most easily discarded by separating it into seven groups.

Key to Groups of *Rhodophyllus*
1. Symmetrical spores
    2. Cap depressed, context thin ....Group 1
    2. Cap not depressed or only so at maturity
        3. Cap conic to papillate ....Group 2
        3. Cap not as above
            4. Cap umbilicate ....Group 4
            4. Cap conic-campanulate to plane ....Group 5
1. Asymmetrical spores
    5. Cap squamulose, fibrillose or fibrous ....Group 7
    5. Cap glabrous
        6. Gills subfree to sinuate ....Group 6
        6. Gills decurrent or adnate ....Group 3

Groups 1, 2, 3, and 4 have no poisonous species. Group 5 has three, *R. nidorosus, R. rhodopolius,* and *R. strictior.* All have non-decurrent gills, hygrophanous caps and non-yellow gills. *R. nidorosus* has a convex gray cap, ovate angular spores, and a nitrous acid odour which separates it from other species. The other two species are separated from others in this group by their brown and gray colour and lack of a mealy odour. *R. rhodopolius* has a campanulate to plane, brown to gray cap, and subglobose angular spores. The cap of *R. strictior* is campanulate to umbonate, cinnamon to gray, and the spores are elongate, angular, and curving.

Group 6 has two poisonous species, *R. murraii* and *R. salmoneum.* These two are divided from nearly all other species in this group by their yellow to orange-red pigment. *R. salmoneum* is conical to campanulate, salmon-coloured, with nearly square spores. *R. murraii* is rare. Do not confuse these with the orange *Hygrophori* which have white spores.

Group 7 has one poisonous species, *R. sinuatus.* It is characterized by 1) mealy odour and taste; 2) cap soapy when wet, silky when dry; and 3) sordid brown to grayish cap. This species integrates with other larger species and cannot presently be separated easily. It can also be confused with *Tricholoma* and *Lyophyllum,* which have white spores.

Where and When—Three of the species of *Rhodophyllus, R. nidosorus, R. salmoneum,* and *R. strictior* occur summer to fall on sphagnum or decayed wood under trees. *R. sinuatus* is a fall species that appears under conifers or beech, and *R. rhodopolius* grows in summer to fall in deciduous or mixed woods.

Nature of Toxin—Type III, gastrointestinal. Some species may also include hepatotoxin and should be considered very poisonous as deaths have occurred from it.

Rhodophyllus salmoneum (75% actual size)

Paxillus involutus (50% actual size)

Paxillus

Description—*Fruiting Body:* pileate-stipitate or not; *Cap:* fleshy; *Flesh:* firm; *Gills:* decurrent, often anastomosing particularly near stem, easily separable from the cap; *Stem:* central, eccentric, lateral or lacking, neither annulate nor volvate; *Spores:* clay-coloured to chocolate, ovoid, ellipsoid, or oblong, smooth; *Gill Trama:* bilateral.

Distinguishing Features—1) brown spores; 2) decurrent gills; and 3) gills easily separable from stem.

Remarks—Among the brown-spored genera, there are only a few other than *Paxillus* that have decurrent gills. None of these have readily separable gills. Also, *Crepidotus* has an eccentric stem. *Galerina* and *Tubaria* are very small, non-fleshy mushrooms, and *Gymnopilus* is brightly coloured, usually with a yellow stem.

Name Derivation—*Paxillus* means a small stake.

Poisonous Species—*P. involutus* is the only poisonous member of this genus. It is characterized by a lateral, eccentric or central glabrous stem, the presence of cystidia and clamp connections, and absence of a veil. The cap is yellow-brown to red-brown with an inrolled margin. The other common species, *P. atrotomentosus*, has an eccentric stem covered with dense black hairs.

Where and When—*P. atrotomentosus* occurs on old stumps, generally under conifers in summer and fall, while *P. involutus* grows on the ground in open woods or lawns, summer and fall.

Nature of Toxin—Type III, gastrointestinal. This should be considered as dangerous, since some deaths have been reported from it. The toxin is apparently most potent in raw specimens. Other authorities cite poisoning by this species from a gradually acquired allergic sensitivity that can one day suddenly lead to severe hemolysis, shock and acute kidney failure following a meal of *P. involutus*, resembling type Ib.

Agaricus

Description—*Fruiting Body:* pluteoid; *Cap:* fleshy; *Epicutis:*

of appressed, filamentous hyphae or fragments of a palisade; *Flesh:* often staining yellow or red when bruised; *Gills:* free, first white or pink and later purple-brown; *Stem:* central, annulate, not volvate, fleshy; *Spores:* chocolate to purple-brown, subglobose, ovoid, oblong, or ellipsoid, smooth; *Gill Trama:* regular; *Clamp Connections:* usually absent.

Distinguishing Features—1) free gills; 2) annulus; and 3) chocolate to purple-brown spores.

Remarks—It would be very difficult to mix this genus up with any other, as no other brown-spored genera has free gills and an annulus. *Stropharia, Psilocybe,* and *Naematoloma* may have an annulus and purple-brown gills, but the gills are attached. Mushrooms most resembling *Agaricus* are the white-spored *Amanita* and *Lepiota,* or the pink-spored *Chamaeota.*

Name Derivation—*Agaricus* is from agarocon, a Greek word for fungus.

Poisonous Species—Six species of *Agaricus* have been reported as poisonous or poisonous to some people. Reports of gastrointestinal disturbances occur for *A. albolutescens, A. xanthodermus, A. sylvicola, A. arvensis* var. *palustris, A. placomyces,* and *A. hondensis.* Four of these, *A. albolutescens, A. xanthodermus, A. sylvicola,* and *A. arvensis* resemble each other closely and also resemble three edible species. *A. sylvicola* is characterized by a white fibrillose cap, dull pink gills which become chocolate brown, conspicuous annulus with yellow floccose patches on the underside, and elongate stem with flattened base. It sometimes turns yellow slowly when bruised, smells of almond, and grows in the woods. *A. arvensis* var. *palustris* differs mainly in having larger spores and growing in swamps, fields and meadows. *A. albolutescens* and *A. xanthodermus* stain deep to amber yellow immediately on bruising. The cap of A. albolutescens finally becomes all yellow with age, while *A. xanthodermus* smells of creosote.

These four could be confused with the non-poisonous species

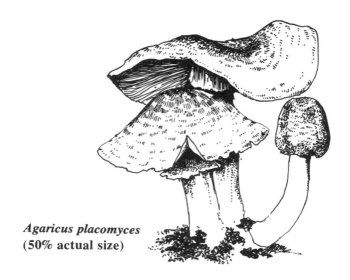

Agaricus placomyces
(50% actual size)

Agaricus sylvicola
(50% actual size)

A. campestris, A. rodmanii, A. benesii, or *A. abruptibulbus. A. campestris* differs in having a single, thin, membranous annulus which is frequently evanescent and a short stem. *A. benesii* differs in bruising red, and *A. abruptibulbus* in being more slender and having a conspicuous abrupt bulb.

A. hondensis and *A. placomyces* have pigmented fruiting bodies and a stem that is glabrous below the annulus when young. *A. placomyces* can be identified by the wood-brown, gray, or black fibrils on its very flat cap, creosote odour, and habit of growing in clusters. *A. hondensis* generally lacks fibrils, but is white when young becoming vinaceous when old. It smells of creosote and has a soapy metallic flavour.

These last two resemble *A. silvaticus,* a non-poisonous species. It, however, has reddish fibrils and no odour.

Where and When—Identification of *Agaricus sp.* is often based on habitat. All of the species mentioned usually occur in summer and fall but do occasionally occur in the spring. *A. arvensis* var. *palustris* is the only one found in swamps, although it also occurs in meadows. Woodland species are *A. abruptibulbus, A. placomyces, A. sylvicola, A. xanthodermus,* and *A. albolutescens. A. campestris* and *A. rodmanii* are found in pastures and lawns.

Nature of Toxin—Type III, gastrointestinal.

Hebeloma   Colour Plate XV

Description—*Fruiting Body:* stipitate-pileate; *Cap:* viscid; *Epicutis:* of thin gelatinous filaments; *Flesh:* usually white; *Gills:* adnexed to emarginate, pallid to pale brown initially, becoming darker brown often with white edge; *Stem:* central, fleshy to fleshy-fibrillose, white at least at apex, apex usually pruinose or squamulose, with or without annulus, no volva; *Spores:* clay-coloured to vinaceous brown, ellipsoid, oblong or fusiform, usually rough; *Gill Trama:* regular; *Clamp Connections:* present; *Cheilocystidia:* hyaline, distinct and crowded often giving gills a white edge; *Habitat:* terrestrial.

Distinguishing Features—1) clay-coloured spores; 2) fleshy central stem; 3) adnexed to emarginate gills; and 4) viscid cap.

Remarks—*Hebeloma* resembles *Cortinarius, Inocybe,* or *Pholiota* most closely in the field. *Cortinarius* has a definite cobwebby veil. If *Hebeloma* has a veil, it is fibrillose. The viscid cap distinguishes it from *Inocybe* and *Pholiota.* It is larger and more fleshy than *Galerina* which is also usually seen with decurrent gills.

Name Derivation—*Hebeloma* is derived from hebe, dull or blunt, and loma, margin.

Poisonous Species—Two or possibly three species of *Hebeloma* may be poisonous. Records of poisonings occur for *H. crustuliniforme, H. fastibile,* and *H. sinapizans.* However, there has been speculation that reports of poisoning of *H. crustuliniforme* and *H. sinapizans* may be confused. Both should be considered poisonous until this is clarified. All three of these have dull tawny to clay-coloured spores and belong to the subgenus *Hebeloma,* as opposed to the subgenus *Porphypolema,* which has reddish to pink-brown spores. *H. fastibile* has a distinct veil in young specimens, while *H. crustuliniforme* and *H. sinapizans* do not. *H. fastibile* has a yellowish-tan convex to plane cap, and the gills are beaded with drops of liquid in wet weather. These features separate it from *H. mesophaeum* with its dull yellow conical cap, and *H. pascuense* with its convex-umbonate rust-coloured cap. *H. crustuliniforme* can be separated by its stuffed or hollow stem from *H. sinapizans,* which has a solid stem.

Where and When—*H. fastibile, H. mesophaeum,* and *H. sinapizans* are usually found in the fall in moist lowland woods with sandy soil. *H. crustuliniforme* occurs in the fall in mixed conifer and deciduous or conifer woods, and often grows in fairy rings. *H. pascuense* grows spring, summer, and fall in pastures and open woods.

Nature of Toxin—Probably Type IIb, muscarine; poisoning mild unless the mushrooms are parboiled, which makes them edible.

Galerina   Colour Plates XVI-XVII

Description—*Fruiting Body:* mycenoid or rarely collybioid to somewhat fleshy or fleshy fragile; *Cap:* hygrophanous, margin appressed to stem in button stages, becoming conical to campanulate or nearly plane at maturity; *Epicutis:* a dense layer of narrow appressed hyphae; *Gills:* adnexed, adnate, or decurrent, usually white-fringed; *Stem:* central, slender, brittle, annulate or not, not volvate; *Spores:* rusty, usually ornamented with a plage, variously shaped; *Gill Trama:* regular to slightly irregular; *Cheilocystidia:* present.

Distinguishing Features—1) rust-coloured spores; 2) slender brittle stem; 3) filamentous cuticle; and 4) appressed cap margin when young.

Remarks—The small size of *Galerina* immediately separates it from the more fleshy brown-spored Agarics. Indeed, it would be more easily confused with the white-spored *Mycena* or *Marasmius*, or the black-spored *Panaeolus*. Among the smaller brown-spored mushrooms, *Galerina* could be confused with *Psilocybe, Bolbitius, Agrocybe, Conocybe, Tubaria,* or *Inocybe*. Of these, *Bolbitius, Agrocybe* and *Conocybe* all have a cellular cuticle, not a fibrous one. *Psilocybe* has purple-brown spores, and *Inocybe* is larger, has a fibrillose cap, and an incurved cap margin at first. *Tubaria* has clamp connections on the hyphae and lacks the white fringe on the gills caused by cheilocystidia.

Name Derivation—*Galerina* is derived from galerus, a cap.

Poisonous Species—*Galerina* is a large genus of tiny brown mushrooms that simply cannot be separated on field characteris-

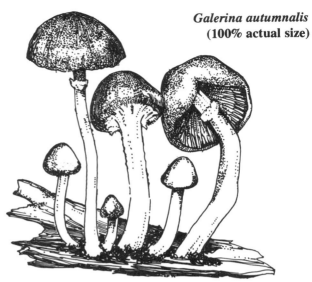

Galerina autumnalis
(100% actual size)

Hebeloma crustuliniforme
(100% actual size)

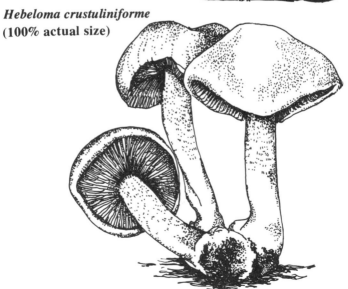

Colour Plate I
Tricholoma saponaceum

Colour Plate II
Hygrophorus conicus

Colour Plate III   *Mycena galericulata*

Colour Plate IV   *Clitocybe dealbata*

Colour Plate V   *Lyophyllum multiceps*

Colour Plate VI   Colour Plate VII
Russula emetica   *Lactarius torminosus*

Colour Plate VIII
Lactarius scrobiculatus

Colour Plate IX
Amanita muscaria

Colour Plate X
Amanita gemmata

Colour Plate XI
Amanita pantherina

Colour Plate XII
Amanita pantherina
Cap and annulus detail.

Colour Plate XIII   *Rhodophylus strictius*

Colour Plate XIV   *Paxillus involutus*

Colour Plate XV   *Hebeloma crustuliniforme*

Colour Plate XVI
Galerina autumnalis

Colour Plate XVII
Galerina sp.

One of the many *Galerina* species of unknown toxicity which superficially resemble some *Psilocybe*.

Colour Plate XVIII
Cortinarius sanguineus

A member of the dangerous subgenus Dermocybe.

Colour Plate XIX   *Inocybe fastigiata*

Colour Plate XX   *Phaeolepiota aurea*

Colour Plate XXI · *Gomphus floccosus*

Colour Plate XXII · *Psilocybe stuntzii*

Colour Plate XXIII
Psilocybe semilanceata
Fresh versus hygrophanus form.

Colour Plate XXIV
Psilocybe semilanceata
In habitat.

Colour Plate XXV
Psilocybe strictipes

Colour Plate XXVI *Psilocybe cubensis*

Colour Plate XXVII
Psilocybe baeocystis

Colour Plate XXIX
Naemataloma fasciculare

Colour Plate XXVIII
Psilocybe pelliculosa

Colour Plate XXX
Coprinus atramentarius

Colour Plate XXXI
Panaeolus campanulatus

Colour Plate XXXII
Gyromitra esculenta

Colour Plate XXXIII
Gyromitra infula

Colour Plate XXXIV
Helvella lacunosa

Colour Plate XXXV
Peziza venosa

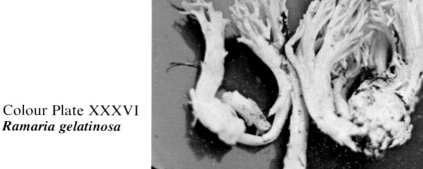

Colour Plate XXXVI
Ramaria gelatinosa

tics. The genus is divided into nine sections based almost entirely on microscopic features.

Key to Groups of *Galerina*

1. Spores calyptrate . . . . .Group 1
1. Spores non-calyptrate
   2. Cap dry or, if moist and hygrophanous, then innately fibrillose when faded or with coloured fibrils over margin of pileus . . . . .Group 2
   2. Not as above
      3. Pleurocystidia present
         4. Spores smooth . . . . .Group 3
         4. Spores ornamented
            5. Pleurocystidia thick-walled in neck and ventricose portion . . . . .Group 4
            5. Pleurocystidia thin-walled in neck and ventricose portion
               6. Pleurocystidia with broadly rounded apices . . . . .Group 5
               6. Pleurocystidia with acute to obtuse apices
                  7. Cap margin incurved at first . . . . . . .Group 6
                  7. Cap margin straight at first . . . . . . .Group 7
      3. Pleurocystidia absent
         8. Spores with narrow apical pore . . . . .Group 8
         8. Spores lacking apical pore . . . . .Group 9

All three poisonous species of *Galerina* belong in Group 6. However, species in this section without a veil or with calyptrate spores can be eliminated as non-poisonous. *Galerina autumnalis* is characterized by a viscid yellow-brown cap, dark brown stem and gills, narrow white ring, and habit of growing on wood. *G. marginata* has a moist cinnamon-brown stem, pruinose above fibrillose annulus. *G. venenata* has a moist, glabrous cinnamon-brown cap fading to whitish. The stem is brown and it has a thin apical annulus.

Where and When—All three poisonous species of *Galerina* can occur early summer to fall in a wet year. *G. autumnalis* grows on or near wood, while *G. venenata* and *G. marginata* grow in lawns, pastures, or open woods.

Nature of Toxin—Type Ia, cyclopeptide toxins. These *Galerina species* produce the same deadly delayed syndrome as caused by the *Amanita* cyclopeptide toxins.

Cortinarius Colour Plate XVIII

Description—*Fruiting Body:* stipitate-pileate, fleshy; *Cap:* fleshy; *Epicutis:* of filamentous hyphae; *Gills:* subfree to decurrent, narrow or broad, variously coloured; *Stem:* central with cobwebby cortina, no volva; *Spores:* yellow-brown to cinnamon-brown, of various shapes, wrinkly rough; *Gill Trama:* regular; *Habitat:* usually terrestrial.

Distinguishing Features—1) brown spores; and 2) cobwebby partial veil.

Remarks—*Cortinarius* is such a variable genus that it is hard to describe, yet relatively easy to identify. Nine other genera also have brown spores, a veil, and a fibrous cuticle. Of these, only *Gymnopilus* has a cobwebby veil. It can be identified by its orange spore deposit, lignicolous habit, and bright colours. Of the other eight, *Galerina* and *Tubaria* are noticeably much smaller. *Galerina* has white-edged gills and spores either calyptrate or with a plage, and *Tubaria* has thin-walled spores. *Pholiota* and *Inocybe* have smooth spores. *Rozites* has a double veil, and *Phaeolepiota* a broadly flaring one. *Hebeloma* must be separated by a combination of characteristics. It has a viscid cap, clay-coloured spores, and abundant cheilocystidia.

Name Derivation—*Cortinarius* is derived from the word cortina, a veil or curtain.

Poisonous Species

Key to Major Groups of *Cortinarius*

1. Gelatinizing universal veil present; stem viscid . . . . .Group 1
1. Universal veil, if present, not gelatinizing; stem moist or dry
   2. Carpophore reacts black with potassium hydroxide
      3. Cap covered by universal veil when young . . . . . . .Group 2
         (subgenus Dermocybe)
      3. Not as above; cap usually squamulose tomentose . . . . .Group 3
         (subgenus Cortinarius)
   2. Not as above
      4. Cap cuticle of narrow mucilaginous hyphae . . . . . . .Group 4
      4. Hyphae of cuticle not mucilaginous, broad or both broad and narrow
         5. Cap not hygrophanous; cuticle hyphae broad . . . . .Group 5
         5. Cap hygrophanous; cuticle hyphae thick and thin . . . . .Group 6

One species, *C. orellanus,* is known to be poisonous, but all in the subgenus Dermocybe and some in the subgenus Cortinarius are inedible or suspect. The subgenus Dermocybe, which contains *C. orellanus*, is distinguished by a dry cap which is initially covered by a universal veil. The cap is initally subglobose or conic with an involute margin, and later convex-umbonate. The gills are yellow, orange-red, or red, sinuate-adnate, and have serrulate edges. The stem is equal to clavate, the taste bitter, and the mushroom turns black when put in contact with potassium hydroxide.

The subgenus Cortinarius has a dry squamulose tomentose cap surface, is violet, olive-green, yellow, or yellow-brown, has subglobose, elongate to broadly amygdaliform spores, and blackens with potassium hydroxide.

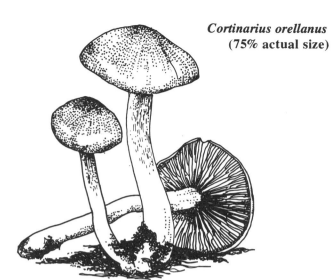

Cortinarius orellanus
(75% actual size)

Inocybe pudica
(100% actual size)

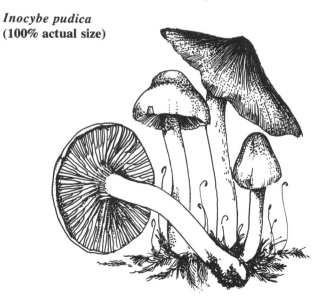

Where and When—*C. orellanus* usually is found in the fall under conifers, but it has not yet been reported in North America. **Nature of Toxin**—Similar to type Ia. The toxin is a polypeptide which has an incubation period of 3-14 days or longer. The exact chemical nature of the toxin is not known but the site of activity is confined to the kidneys. Reported fatality rate in Europe is 10-20%.

Inocybe   Colour Plate XIX

Description—*Fruiting Body:* stipitate-pileate; *Cap:* fibrillose, fibrils running radially, often splitting radially, sometimes scaly to squamulose, dry; *Epicutis:* of filamentous hyphae arranged radially; *Flesh:* firm, often with a strong odour; *Gills:* adnexed, sinuate, or adnate, usually with a paler edge; *Stem:* central, fibrous-fleshy to fleshy, pruinose, with fibrillose annulus or none; *Spores:* clove-brown to almost rusty, smooth, echinulate or with compound warts, angular or nodulose; *Gill Trama:* regular; *Cystidia and Clamp Connections:* present.

Distinguishing Features—1) brown spores; 2) dry fibrillose cap; 3) fibrous-fleshy pruinose stem; and 4) adnexed or adnate gills.

Remarks—*Inocybe* is another genus easily recognized in the field, but hard to differentiate in writing from other genera. *Psilocybe* can be separated by its purple spores, and *Panaeolus* by its black ones. Of the brown-spored genera with fibrillose caps, *Hebeloma* can be identified by its viscid cap; *Galerina* by its generally smaller size, either calyptrate spores or spores with a plage and smooth cap; and *Tubaria* by its small size and thin-walled spores. *Cortinarius* and *Gymnopilus* have a cobwebby veil, while *Phaeolepiota* has a wide flaring veil and *Rozites* a double veil. *Pholiota* has a dry cap surface also, but it has large, coarse scales and lacks the radiating lines of *Inocybe*.

Name Derivation—*Inocybe* in Greek comes from two words meaning fibre and head.

Poisonous Species—*Inocybe* species can be divided into two groups using spore features. The first group has smooth, ellipsoid, fusoid, cylindric, or ovoid spores. The second has nodular, angular, or spiny-stellate spores. Group 1 has at least four poisonous species, *I. fastigiata, I. geophylla, I. lacera,* and *I. pudica. I. geophylla* has a white to tan silky glossy cap, white gills and stem, non-reddening flesh, pleurocystidia, and a weak or spermatic odour. *I. pudica* differs by having a reddening flesh. The only absolute identification can be made by checking for the smooth reniform spores and fusoid ventricose pleurocystidia.

I. fastigiata has a smoky yellow conic-campanulate cap with a broad umbo which splits radially. The gills are white to gray and the stem white or smoky. Its spores are also smooth and reniform.

I. lacera has tuberculate, spiny spores, and a gray-brown fibrillose scaly cap with a brown umbo. The gills are white, becoming cinnamon, and the stem white becoming brown below. The stem flesh is reddening. This last feature separates it from *I. infelix.*

Group 2 has two common poisonous species. The cap of *I. napipes* is dark brown with a silvery artificial-looking coating. It is bell-shaped to flat with a pronounced umbo, smooth, soapy when wet and silky when dry. The gills are white, then grayish. The stem is pale above, brown below with a turnip-like base. This base distinguishes it from other species.

I. decipiens has a cap that is yellow to cinnamon-brown, convex with an umbo. The gills and stem are white, then brown. The spores are angular-tuberculate and pleurocystidia fusoid-ventricose with elongated necks.

Where and When—*I. fastigiata* and *I. geophylla* grow summer and fall in lawns and woods. *I. napipes* and *I. pudica* are found under conifers in the fall. *I. infelix* occurs in wet woods in summer, while *I. lacera* occurs on sandy soil in fall.

Nature of Toxin—Type IIb, muscarine; the amount of toxin differs from species to species.

Phaeolepiota   Colour Plate XX

Description—*Fruiting Body:* stipitate-pileate; *Cap:* fleshy, covered with loose mealy substance consisting of sphaerocysts; *Flesh:* thick, firm; *Gills:* adnexed; *Stem:* central, fleshy, thick, covered with mealy substance, annulate; *Annulus:* broad, flaring, membranous, covered with mealy substance; *Spores:* yellow-brown, smooth or punctate, elongate, nonamyloid; *Gill Trama:* regular; *Clamp Connections:* present.

Distinguishing Features—1) brown spores; 2) broad, flaring annulus; and 3) mealy covering on cap, stem, and annulus.

Remarks—This is a distinct genus that resembles no other. *Cystoderma* is mealy but is white-spored. No other brown-spored genera has either the mealy covering or the flaring membranous annulus.

Name Derivation—*Phaeolepiota* comes from phaeo, dark, lepi, scale and ota, ear.

Potentially Poisonous Species—*P. aurea* is poisonous only to some people, for others it is quite good. This is an easy mushroom to identify. It has a large (10-35 cm in width) light gold cap, yellow-brown gills, and a brown fibrous stipe with an annulus. The whole mushroom is covered with a powdery material that rubs off when dry. No other mushroom resembles this. *P. aurea* is frequently included under *Pholiota*.

Where and When—*P. aurea* usually occurs in the fall on ground under Douglas fir or alder.

Nature of Toxin—Type III, gastrointestinal.

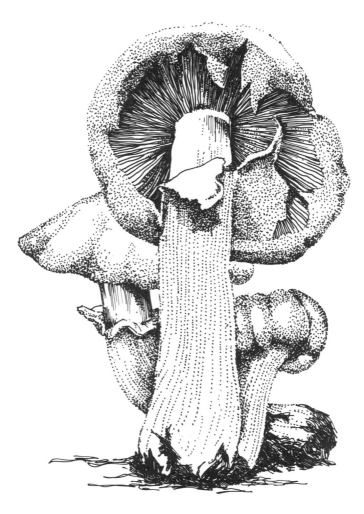

Phaeolepiota aurea (**50% actual size**)

Gomphus   Colour Plate XXI

Description—*Fruiting Body:* stipitate-pileate, thick, fleshy, infundibuliform or tubular; *Cap:* fleshy, often scaly; *Flesh:* whitish; *Gills:* decurrent, ridgiform, forked; *Stem:* fleshy, short, expanding into cap; *Spores:* ochre, ovoid to ellipsoid, usually tuberculate or reticulate.

Distinguishing Features—1) ridge-like gills; and 2) ochre-coloured spores with ornamentations.

Remarks—*Gomphus* is included in most works under *Cantharellus*. They are very similar, both having an infundibuliform to tubular shape and ridge-like gills. *Gomphus* differs mainly in having ochre, ornamented spores.

Name Derivation—*Gomphus* means a wooden bolt or nail.

Poisonous Species—*Gomphus* has only one poisonous species, *G. floccosus*. It is characterized by a funnel-shaped yellow to reddish-orange floccose scaly cap, and a short glabrous ochraceous stem. *Cantharellus kauffmanii* resembles *G. floccosus*, but its scales are brownish, never orange or yellow.

Where and When—*G. floccosus* occurs summer and fall under conifers.

Nature of Toxin—*Gomphus floccosus* contains nor-caperotic acid, causing gastrointestinal discomfort (Type III) in some people.

Conocybe

Description—*Fruiting Body:* mycenoid; *Cap:* hygrophanous, often transparently striate, glistening when dry; *Epicutis:* cellular to hymeniform; *Gills:* attached, usually at first ascendant; *Stem:* slender, at first appressed to cap margin, not annulate or volvate, often pruinose; *Spores:* deep rust, smooth or faintly verrucose, lemon-shaped, ellipsoid, or lentiform, with apical pore; *Gill Trama:* reduced to a few filamentous hyphae flanked by large

71

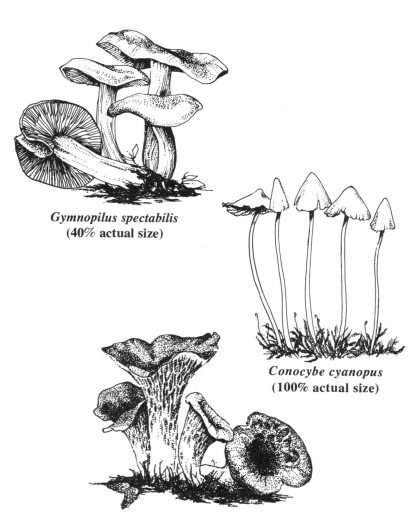

Gymnopilus spectabilis
(40% actual size)

Conocybe cyanopus
(100% actual size)

Gomphus floccosus **(25% actual size)**

swollen cells; *Cheilocystidia:* always present; *Clamp Connections:* usually present.

Distinguishing Features—1) rusty brown spores; 2) cellular cuticle; and 3) thin flesh.

Remarks—The cellular epicutis of *Conocybe* separates it from most other small brown-spored mushrooms such as *Galerina* and *Tubaria.* Only *Agrocybe* and *Bolbitius* have the cellular cuticle. *Bolbitius* has a viscid cap and is autodeliquescent. *Agrocybe* is harder to separate. It is slightly larger (flesh thicker than 3mm) and has buff to clove brown spores rather than rust-coloured ones. *Psilocybe, Panaeolus,* and *Mycena* also superficially resemble *Conocybe,* but have fibrillar cuticles and purple, black, and white spores respectively.

Name Derivation—*Conocybe* means cone head.

Poisonous Species—This genus has two common poisonous species, *C. cynaopus* and *C. filaris. C. cyanopus* can be distinguished from other species by its hollow blue stem. Other features are a cap that is cinnamon and striate when wet, becoming buff and membranous when dry, and cinnamon gills with floccose edges. *C. filaris* has an ochraceus cap with a striate margin, yellow to tan gills when young and a persistent annulus. *C. cyanopus* is sometimes known as *Pholiotina cyanopoda* in other references and *C. filaris* is *Pholiota filaris* in some other references.

Where and When—*C. cyanopus* occurs on moss in wet areas in summer.

Nature of Toxin—Type IIc, psilocybin/psilocin in *C. cyanopus* and type Ia, cyclopeptide toxins in *C. filaris.*

Gymnopilus

Description—*Fruiting Body:* stipitate-pileate, fleshy; *Cap:* brightly coloured; *Epicutis:* formed by hyphal chains which are frequently erect; *Gills:* adnexed to decurrent, broad or narrow, becoming rusty when dried; *Stem:* central, usually yellow, always as long as diameter of cap, annulate or not, never volvate; *Spores:* bright orange-brown, ellipsoid, warty; *Gill Trama:* regular; *Clamp*

Connections: present; *Cystidia:* always present on edge of gills; *Habitat:* lignicolous.

Distinguishing Features—1) orange-brown spores; 2) brightly coloured cap; 3) yellow stem; and 4) lignicolous habitat.

Remarks—Although *Gymnopilus* tends to be a distinct genus, it could be confused with some species of *Cortinarius.* It can usually be distinguished by its bright colours, lignicolous habit, and bitter taste. Another interesting feature of *Gymnopilus* is that it can be grown in culture, whereas *Cortinarius,* a mycorrhizial genus, cannot.

Name Derivation—Gymno means naked, pilus means cap.

Poisonous Species—One common species of *Gymnopilus, G. spectabilis,* is considered poisonous. It is distinguished by 1) large size (9-18 cm broad); 2) clustered habit on conifer wood; 3) bitter taste; 4) spores 8-10 microns long; and 5) cap which becomes squamulose in age. The cap is light yellow-orange to deep orange, the gills pale to medium yellow, and the stem, its flesh, and annulus pale yellow. The spores are zinc-orange.

Where and When—*G. spectabilis* can be found spring and summer on wood under conifers or in the open.

Nature of Toxin—Type IIc, not psilocybin/psilocin, probably baeocystin and/or norbaeocystin.

Psilocybe   Colour Plates XXII-XXVIII

Description—*Fruiting Body:* stipitate-pileate; *Cap:* conic, convex, campanulate, or mammiform, often with fibrillose remains of veil; *Epicutis:* of narrow filamentous hyphae somewhat gelatinized; *Gills:* adnexed to adnate, often with decurrent tooth, usually broad; *Stem:* central, annulate or not; *Flesh:* often bluing; *Spores:* lilac to purple-brown, ovoid, ellipsoid, or oblong, smooth with germ pore; *Gill Trama:* regular or irregular; *Chrysocystidia:* absent; *Clamp Connections:* present.

Distinguishing Features—1) purplish spores; 2) conic to campanulate cap; and 3) veil as traces on cap margin.

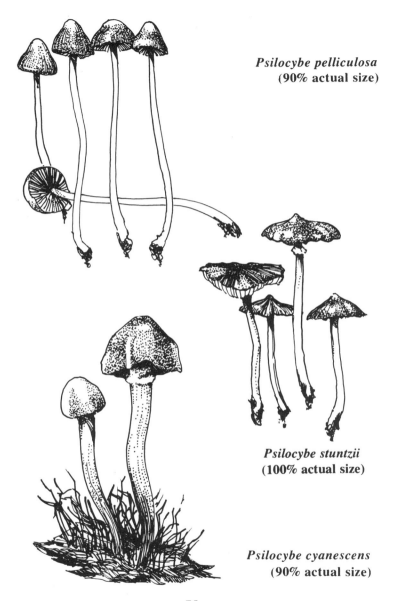

Psilocybe pelliculosa
(90% actual size)

Psilocybe stuntzii
(100% actual size)

Psilocybe cyanescens
(90% actual size)

Remarks—*Psilocybe*, being a frequently hunted mushroom, should be identified carefully. It could easily be confused with *Galerina*, which can be fatal if eaten. However, *Galerina* has brown spores. It could also be confused with the black-spored *Panaeolus* and possibly brown-spored *Inocybe, Pholiota, Hebeloma, Agrocybe,* or *Conocybe.* So be sure to check spore colour. Four other genera have purplish spores. Of these, *Agaricus* has free gills, and *Naematoloma* is brightly coloured and has chrysocystidia. *Stropharia* can usually be separated by the presence of a glutinous annulus, very large spores, and frequently viscid stem. *Psathyrella* has a cellular cuticle.

One other mushroom, a species of *Omphalina* has been recently reported as poisonous by people mistakenly eating it for *Psilocybe.* It has white spores, decurrent gills, an orange trumpet-shaped cap, and grows in pastures. Final evaluation of its toxicity and positive identification studies have not been completed.

Name Derivation—*Psilocybe* is Greek for naked head.

Poisonous Species—

Key to Common *Psilocybe* Species With Bluing Flesh

1. Cap margin straight when young or almost so; habit mycenoid
    2. Cap with a thick and separable pellicle; growing in rotting wood or litter ....*P. pelliculosa*
    2. Pellicle, if present not separable, growing in lawns and pastures ....*P. semilanceata*
1. Cap margin incurved when young; habit collybioid
    3. Persistent annulus present
        4. Growing in dung, robust specimens 21-26 cm tall, cap yellow (native to semitropical areas) ....*P. cubensis*
        4. Growing in lawns and pastures, 5-10 cm tall, cap chestnut brown ....*P. stuntzii*
    3. Annulus if present evanescent
        5. Growing in conifer woodchip mulch; cap and stem staining deep blue when bruised,

flesh of stem staining brown . . . . *P. strictipes*
5. Growing in open lawns; cap and stem stain-
    ing blue-green when bruised, flesh of stem
    not staining brown . . . . *P. baeocystis*

Psilocybe is a large genus, presently in great need of taxonomic work. The first edition of this book misidentified the then undescribed new species *P. stuntzii* as *P. cyanescens*. *P. cyanescens* is a different mushroom which is closer to *P. strictipes*. Taxonomists are now showing great interest in this once neglected group. We showed *Psilocybe* authority Gaston Guzman (who, with Jonathan Ott, named *P. stuntzii*) variations of *P. stuntzii* that clearly did not fit the species description. We suspect when the research on these mushrooms is completed we will find that each recognized species is actually a member of a considerably larger swarm of now undescribed species.

The mycenoid *Psilocybe* species with a blue staining reaction are *P. semilanceata* and *P. pelliculosa*. Both are similar side by side, but have entirely different habitats. *P. pelliculosa* occurs in rotting wood and has an easily separable cuticle. *P. semilanceata* occurs in tall, rank grass. Both species are common and have low potency. Twenty to forty mushrooms will cause a definite intoxication. The lanceolate or campanulate cap shape is frequently used to recognize *P. semilanceata* in the field but this mushroom actually ranges from almost plane to hemispheric as well.

The collybioid species of *Psilocybe* are easy to differentiate on the basis of form and habitat. First the oddball—*P. cubensis*, a native of semi-tropical areas, occurs on dung. It is presently appearing in northern areas because it is quite easy to cultivate. *P. cubensis* is a very large, stropharioid mushroom with a conspicuous ring. On a gram for gram basis, it is considered relatively weak, about the same as *P. stuntzii*. *P. stuntzii* occurs in lawns and pastures, not quite as commonly as *P. semilanceata*. The chestnut-brown cap and blue staining floccose ring distinguish it from other *Psilocybe* species. Twenty to forty specimens of fresh

P. stuntzii or *P. semilanceata* (or 10 to 20 of each of these species taken in combination together), or one to three of *P. cubensis*, will cause a definite intoxication. Drying decreases potency about in half.

Psilocybe strictipes has a hygrophanous yellow-brown or olive-brown cap, and a stem flesh which tends to turn brown when broken. It is somewhat gregarious and occurs commonly in conifer bark, especially bark mulch in flower beds. *P. baeocystis* is darker in colour when fresh, deep olive-brown which fades to a beautiful oyster gray on drying. The stem flesh does not show brown staining tendency when bruised. This mushroom occurs rarely in lawns. Both mushrooms are **very potent**. Occasionally, persons accustomed to collecting *P. semilanceata* discover some *P. baeocystis* or *P. strictipes*. One could have an interesting evening with twenty to forty *P. semilanceata* but this many *P. baeocystis* and possibly *P. strictipes* would be a dangerous overdose. Two specimens of *P. baeocystis* and four of *P. strictipes* is an effective dose. The only death attributed to a hallucinogenic *Psilocybe* was a child in Washington who ate *P. baeocystis*. Recent observations on special sensitivity in children are discussed on page 107.

Occasionally we have eaten these mushrooms, as discussed on page 112. Since many people have recently been seeking these mushrooms for the same purpose, we recommend the following procedure after the mushroom is properly identified:

1. Carefully graduate your dose day by day, beginning with one mushroom, then progressing to three, and then to ten.

2. Eat them on an empty stomach, since a full stomach tends to dilute the effects.

3. Eat them either fresh in the field or in an omelet, and spend the rest of the day out of doors. Nature's sensory inputs are superior to humanity's artificial environment.

Where and When—All species of *Psilocybe* listed may be found summer and fall as soon as the rains begin. See the key for the type of habitat.

Nature of Toxin—Type IIc, psilocybin/psilocin or baeocystin.

Naematoloma   Colour Plate XXIX

Description—*Fruiting Body:* pileate-stipitate; *Cap:* not hygrophanous, usually of bright colours with an appendiculate veil on the margin; *Epicutis:* of hyaline, filamentous, slightly gelatinized hyphae, hypodermium subcellular; *Gills:* adnexed, adnate, or with decurrent tooth; *Stem:* central, fibrous, rarely annulate, becoming hollow; *Spores:* brown to purple-black; *Cystidia:* present; *Gill Trama:* regular; *Chrysocystidia:* present.

Distinguishing Features—1) purple-black spores; 2) subcellular hypodermium; and 3) chrysocystidia.

Remarks—Three other genera have purple-black spores: of these, *Agaricus* has free gills; *Psilocybe* lacks chrysocystidia, and the hypodermium is not subcellular; and *Stropharia* has a distinct annulus.

Name Derivation—Naemato means filament or thread and loma means border or margin.

Poisonous Species—*N. fasciculare*, the one poisonous species, is one of a group with spores smaller than 10 microns, no annulus, and grows in dense clusters on wood. It has an orange-yellow or green-yellow cap with yellow flesh, yellow gills that become green and then purplish, and a yellow stem. It grows in clusters on dead trees and stumps and tastes bitter.

Resembling *N. fasciculare* is *N. capnoides*. It differs in having smoky-gray gills and lack of bitter taste. Another, *N. sublateritium*, has a brick red cap.

Where and When—All three species listed grow on decaying wood late summer and fall. *N. fasciculare* may also come up in the spring.

Nature of Toxin—Type III, gastrointestinal. In addition, special caution should be given this mushroom since fatal poisonings have been attributed to this mushroom in Italy and Japan. Symptoms and pathology of these cases resembled those produced by type Ia.

79

Coprinus

Description—*Fruiting Body:* stipitate-pileate; *Cap:* usually conic to campanulate when young, occasionally subglobose, then expanding; *Epicutis:* varied, frequently plicate-furrowed along back of gills; *Flesh:* white or whitish, firm, thin, fragile, or almost absent; *Gills:* initially white, later black, free, sinuate, adnexed, or adnate, with parallel sides, usually autodeliquescent; *Stem:* central, straight, annulate, not volvate; *Veil:* if present, double, condensed into annulus, or resembling volva; *Spores:* black or fuscous with germ pore, variously shaped, smooth or ornamented, discolouring in concentrated sulphuric acid; *Cystidia:* characteristically large; *Gill Trama:* regular.

Distinguishing Features—1) black spores; 2) autodeliquescent gills or plicate-striate cap; and 3) parallel gill edges.

Remarks—The gills and often the flesh of *Coprinus* usually dissolve into a black ink after release of spores. No other black-spored genus has this characteristic. One brown-spored genus, *Bolbitius*, does. A few species of *Coprinus* do not autodeliquesce. These have a plicate-striate cap and parallel gill edges, and so are easily distinguished from other black-spored genera.

Name Derivation—*Coprinus* is Greek for dung.

Poisonous Species—One species of *Coprinus*, *C. atramentarius*, has a peculiar type of poisoning that occurs only when it is eaten at a meal wherein an alcoholic beverage is consumed. It has a smooth to innately fibrillose plicate-striate grayish-brown cap without scales or tomentum. The annulus is evanescent. It grows in clusters on ground or wood. This differs from the common *C. comatus*, which has a white scaly cap, and *C. micaceus*, which has a strongly striate cap with glistening particles.

Where and When—*C. atramentarius* and *C. micaceus* grow on decaying wood all year long, while *C. comatus* occurs spring and fall along sandy roadsides and in lawns and pastures.

Nature of Toxin—Type IV, disulphiram like-alcohol reaction.

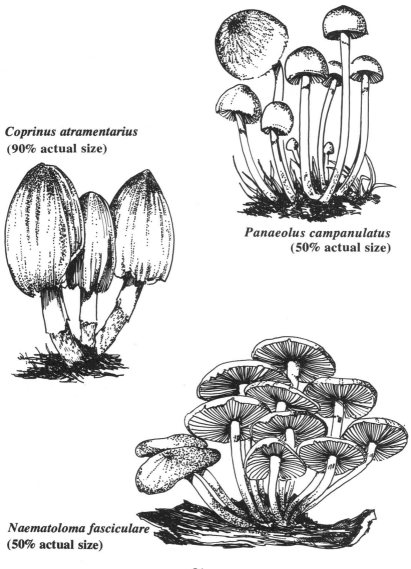

Coprinus atramentarius
(90% actual size)

Panaeolus campanulatus
(50% actual size)

Naematoloma fasciculare
(50% actual size)

Description—*Fruiting Body:* pileate-stipitate; *Cap:* campanulate or conic, usually hygrophanous, neither plicate-striate nor sulcate-striate, often appendiculate with whitish or black-stained veil; *Epicutis:* cellular; *Flesh:* not bluing; *Gills:* attached, mottled due to uneven maturation of spores, not deliquescent, with convergent faces; *Stem:* central, thin, tubular, at least partly pigmented; *Spores:* black, lemon-shaped or ellipsoid with apical pore, smooth; *Cheilocystidia:* present.

Distinguishing Features—1) black spores, non-fading in sulphuric acid; 2) cellular non-striate cap; and 3) mottled gills.

Remarks—*Panaeolus* often appears as a small brown mushroom closely   resembling *Psilocybe, Galerina,* or even possibly *Tubaria, Hebeloma, Inocybe, Pholiota, Conocybe, Agrocybe, Bolbitius, Stropharia, Mycena,* or *Marasmius.* This seems like a lot of confusion, but almost all of these can be eliminated on spore colour. *Mycena* and *Marasmius* have white spores, and *Galerina, Conocybe, Agrocybe, Bolbitius, Tubaria, Hebeloma, Inocybe,* and *Pholiota* have brown spores. *Psilocybe* and *Stropharia* have purple to purple-brown spores. It also differs from *Psilocybe* in having a cellular epicutis, and from *Stropharia* by lacking an annulus.

Panaeolus differs from the other black-spored genera in having mottled gills and spores that retain their colour in concentrated sulphuric acid. *Psathyrella* has spores which decolour in sulphuric acid. *Coprinus* is either plicate-striate or autodeliquescent, and *Chroogomphus* and *Gomphidius* are larger fleshier mushrooms with broad, strongly decurrent gills.

Name Derivation—*Panaeolus* in Greek means all variegated.

Poisonous Species—Three species of *Panaeolus* are sometimes considered to be poisonous. These are *P. sphinctrinus, P. retirugis,* and *P. papilionaceus. P. retirugis* has a gray to clay-coloured reticulately veined cap with parts of a membranous veil adhering to the cap margin, variegated gills with white floccose edges, and a whitish hollow stem tinged red on surface or within. *P. papilionaceus* has a smoky-gray cap with the veil adhering to the margin, variegated gills, and a white hollow stem which is brown at the base. *P. sphinctrinus* has a brown to gray smooth cap with the veil adhering to the margin, variegated gills with white floccose edges, and a reddish-brown hollow pruinose stem. These can be easily separated from two dubious species, *P. solidipes* with a solid stem, and *P. fimicola* with a dark zone at the cap margin. *Panaeolina foenisecii* (sometimes known as *Panaeolus*) can be distinguished by its deep purple fuscous warty spores.

Where and When—All species of this genus, except *P. foenisecii*, grow on dung in spring to fall. *P. foenisecii* grows on irrigated lawns and pastures in summer and fall.

Nature of Toxin—Type IIc, psilocybin/psilocin is present in *Panaeolina foenisecii* only when it occurs on the east coast. The presence of this material in other members of this genus has not yet been completely established.

Boletus

Description—*Fruiting Body:* stipitate-pileate; *Cap:* hemispherical to convex or plane without coarse blackish scales; *Flesh:* firm; *Hymenial Surface:* porose; *Stem:* fleshy, solid, central, or slightly eccentric, not scabrous; *Veil:* absent, or at least not powdery dry and floccose; *Spores:* amber-brown, yellow-brown or olive-brown.

Distinguishing Features—1) non-scaly cap and stem; 2) absence of veil; 3) solid, fleshy stem; 4) amber-brown, olive-brown or yellow-brown spores; and 5) porose hymenium.

Remarks—The fleshy stipitate-pileate fruiting body with a porose hymenium places this genus in the Boletaceae. There are ten genera in this family, nine of which at first glance seem to look alike. Of these nine, *Fuscoboletinus* and *Tylopilus* have gray-brown to pink-brown spores, and *Gyroporus* has pale yellow

Boletus eastwoodiae (75% actual size)

spores. *Pulveroboletus* has a dry, floccose veil, *Strobilomyces* has coarse gray to black scales on the cap, and *Leccinum* has dark scales on the stem. *Boletellus* has longitudinal wings, folds, or striations on the spores. *Suillus* must be identified by a combination of characters. It has two or more of the following features: 1) cap viscid; 2) cap dry and scaly with stem sheathed in veil; 3) gelatinous annulus; or 4) glandular dotted stem.

Name Derivation—*Boletus* is Greek for a clod.

Poisonous Species—The genus *Boletus* has several poisonous species. In general, any specimen with red pores should be suspect. Due to the large number of species, this genus is divided into nine sections, and each section into groups.

Key to Sections

1. Spores ornamented ....Allospori
1. Spores smooth
   2. Spores truncate or notched at apex ....Truncati
   2. Spores not as above
      3. Hymenophore pinkish red when old, taste
        usually acrid, cap viscid or soft ....Piperati
      3. Not as above
        4. Stem reticulate, at least near apex ....Boletus
        4. Stem furfuraceous, pruinose, or
          glabrous
            5. Cap unpolished to velvety or sub-
               tomentose ....Subtomentosi
            5. Cap glabrous and moist or viscid
               6. Stem furfuraceous to punctate,
                  ornamentation not darkening ...Pseudoleccinum
               6. Stem pruinose to naked ....Pseudoboleti

Here we will deal only with the sections with poisonous species, Subtomentosi and Boletus. Section Subtomentosi has one poisonous species, *B. miniato-olivaceus* var. *sensibilis*. It is in subsection Fraterni which is characterized by a red to yellow cap, yellow flesh, tubes which stain blue on injury, and a naked to pruinose stem less than 3 cm thick at the apex. *B. miniato-olivaceus* var. *sensibilis* is separated from related species by broad vesiculose pleurocystidia. It has a red cap, yellow tubes and yellow stem with red stains at base. All parts change to blackish-blue when damaged.

Section Boletus has at least, four poisonous species, all in subsection Luridus. It is distinguished by pores which, when young, are red to dark yellow-green. Three of these species, *B. eastwoodiae, B. luridus,* and *B. satanas,* are very similar. They have orange to red pores, reticulations on the stem, and spores 5-7 microns wide. *B. eastwoodiae* has an olive-brown cap, red and yellow stem, and scarlet tube mouths. *B. luridus* has a yellow-brown cap, red and yellow stem, and scarlet tube mouth. The last species, *B. subvelutipes*, has a pruinose stem, yellow-brown to reddish-brown cap, yellow tubes with brownish-red mouths, and a yellow and red stem. It is divided from related species by having caulocystidia, yellow flesh, large spores, cap drying yellow, and base of stem with red hairs.

Where and When—*B. luridus* and *B. satanas* occur summer and fall in oak woods, while *B. eastwoodiae* grows under conifers in the fall.

Nature of Toxin—Type III, gastointestinal.

Verpa

Description—*Fruiting Body:* stipitate-pileate; *Cap:* bell-shaped to conic, campanulate or cylindric, yellow to dark brown, vertically furrowed, pendulous from apex of stem; *Hymenium:* covering outside of cap; *Stem:* fleshy, cream white, long, hollow.

Distinguishing Features—1) fertile portion with vertical furrows; and 2) lobe edge free of stem.

Remarks—*Verpa* can be distinguished from *Morchella* by the cap which is pendulous from the apex of the stem. *Helvella* has a saddle-shaped cap, and *Gyromitra* and *Neogyromitra* a convoluted cap.

Name Derivation—*Verpa* means a rod.

Poisonous Species—*Verpa bohemica*, a prized edible mushroom, is poisonous to some people. It has a tan to brown thimble-shaped cap attached to the apex of a cream-white stem. This is the only common species of *Verpa*.

Where and When—*Verpa* occurs March to April and occasionally as late as June in cooler areas under cottonwoods.

Nature of Toxin—Type III, gastrointestinal, associated with loss of coordination. Many people eat *Verpa* for years and then suddenly discover that they can no longer tolerate it. Because of this, it should be eaten cautiously.

Neogyromitra

Description—*Fruiting Body:* stipitate-pileate; *Cap:* brown, convoluted, brain-like; *Hymenium:* covering outside of cap; *Stem:* folded and convoluted.

Distinguishing Features—1) brain-like cap; and 2) convoluted stem.

Remarks—*Neogyromitra* has a brain-like cap. This feature separates it from *Verpa, Morchella,* and *Helvella. Gyromitra* differs in having a short chambered stem that is not convoluted.

Name Derivation—Neo means new, gyro to turn and mitra is a head covering.

Potentially Poisonous Species—One common species, *N. gigas*, has an ochre-yellow to tan cap which is 10-24 cm across, and which often comes down over and hides the white convoluted stem. The stem is often nearly as big as the cap. The large size distinguishes this from others in *Neogyromitra, Helvella,* or *Gyromitra*.

87

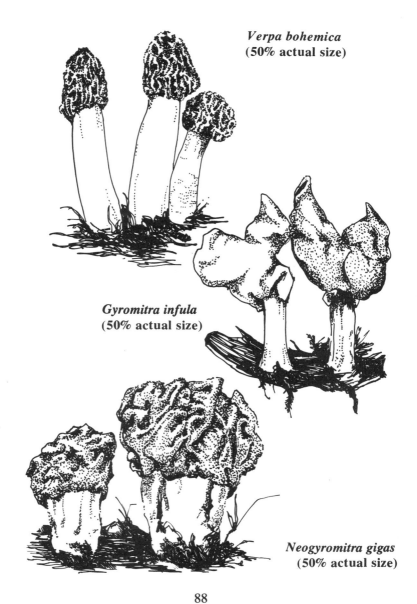

Verpa bohemica
(50% actual size)

Gyromitra infula
(50% actual size)

Neogyromitra gigas
(50% actual size)

88

Where and When—*N. gigas* occurs spring and early summer under conifers.

Nature of Toxin—Type Ib. This mushroom should be parboiled, due to the presence of gyromitrin in the closely related *Gyromitra* species.

Gyromitra   Colour Plates XXXII-XXXIII

Description—*Fruiting Body:* stipitate-pileate; *Cap:* brown, convoluted, brain-like; *Hymenium:* covering outside of cap; *Stem:* short, stout, hollowed, or chambered, often ridged or furrowed, attached to cap at apex and adhering closely and often fused with it.

Distinguishing Features—1) convoluted, brain-like cap; and 2) stout, often chambered, and ridged stem.

Remarks—The convoluted brain-like cap distinguishes *Gyromitra* from *Helvella* with its saddle-shaped cap, and from *Verpa* and *Morchella* with their ridged, pitted cap. *Neogyromitra* differs in having a thick, convoluted stem.

Name Derivation—*Gyromitra* is from gyro, to turn, and mitra, a head covering.

Poisonous Species—Two common species are *G. esculenta* and *G. infula*. *G. esculenta* has a dark reddish-brown cap folded and convoluted like a brain. The stem is white to brownish, attached near the top, smooth or grooved.

G. infula has a cinnamon to dark cap folded back into a saddle shape. The stem is light purple, usually smooth, and the spores are white.

Where and When—Both species occur late summer to fall, on rotting wood under trees or in the open.

Nature of Toxin—Type Ib, gyromitrin. These poisonous species cannot be recommended for eating since fatal poisonings have been reported in spite of parboiling.

Helvella

Description—*Fruiting Body:* stipitate-pileate; *Cap:* saddle-shaped with lobes bent toward stem; *Hymenium:* covering outside of cap; *Stem:* white to gray, attached at apex to fertile portion, long, cylindrical, hollow, or chambered, surface ribbed or furrowed.

Distinguishing Features—1) saddle-shaped fertile portion attached to stem only at apex; and 2) distinct stem.

Remarks—*Helvella* may easily be confused with a number of other genera. Of these, *Verpa* and *Morchella* differ in having definite ridges and pits on the fertile portion, and *Gyromitra* and *Neogyromitra* have a convoluted or irregularly folded fertile portion.

Name Derivation—*Helvella* means a small pot herb.

Potentially Poisonous Species—One common species, *H. lacunosa*, has a white to blackish-gray cap folded back in saddle shape, white spores, and a white or gray stem with longitudinal depressions.

Where and When—*H. lacunosa* is usually found after heavy rains in the fall, under Douglas fir or alder.

Nature of Toxin—Type Ib. All *Helvella species* should be parboiled to remove any possible gyromitrin. Old specimens are reported to be more dangerous than fresh ones.

Peziza

Description—*Fruiting Body:* epigeous from first, cup-shaped, medium to large, not hairy, sessile or with short stalk, fleshy to brittle, yellow to brown-gray or olive; *Spores:* elliptical; *Asci:* stain blue at upper end in iodine solution.

Distinguishing Features—1) cup-shaped; 2) sessile or short stalk; 3) elliptical spores; and 4) bluing asci.

Remarks—There are many sessile cup-shaped fungi, and it really requires a key to separate them well. Some that resemble

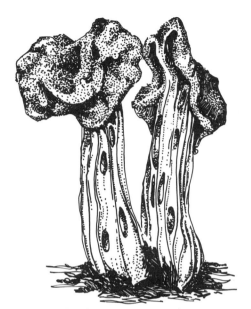

Helvella lacunosa (75% actual size)

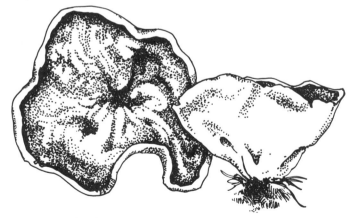

Peziza venosa (100% actual size)

Peziza are *Geopyxis* and *Urnula* which have a split or crenate margin, *Patella* which is discoid, *Paxina* which is tomentose, and *Plicaria* which has globose spores.

Name Derivation—The name *Peziza* was given by Pliny.

Poisonous Species—Some species have been reported as causing slight gastrointestinal upsets, so caution should be used with this genus.

Nature of Toxin—Type III, gastrointestinal.

Ramaria   Colour Plate XXXVI

Description—*Fruiting Body:* fleshy, simple to repeatedly branched, smooth, erect, branch tips rounded or pointed; *Stem:* more or less distinct; *Hymenium:* glabrous, evenly distributed over branches; *Spores:* brown, smooth or rough.

Distinguishing Features—1) coloured spores; 2) branch tips rounded or pointed; and 3) fruiting body fleshy to fragile.

Remarks—*Ramaria* is quite easily separated from the other common coral fungi. *Clavaria* has hyaline spores, *Typhula* arises from a sclerotium, *Clavariadelphus* is simple clubs with expanded apices, *Clavicorona* has truncate to cupulate apices, and *Clavulina* is waxy-fibrous.

Name Derivation—*Ramaria* is from the Greek word ramus, a branch.

Poisonous Species—Two species of *Ramaria* are considered poisonous, *R. gelatinosa* and *R. formosa*. *R. formosa* is pink to rosy pink with yellow branch tips. The flesh is white, pulpy to fibrous, and turns black when bruised. *R. gelatinosa* is cream or pinkish-cinnamon with yellow branch tips. The flesh is semitransparent and gelatinous. This gelatinous flesh separates it from related species. *R. subbotrytis* closely resembles *R. formosa*. It has numerous geranium-pink branches lacking yellow tips growing

Sarcosphaera eximia **(75% actual size)**

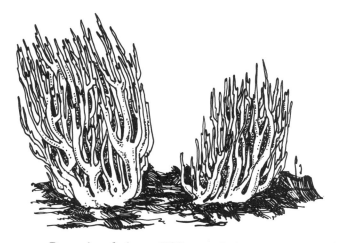

Ramaria gelatinosa **(50% actual size)**

from a large white central base. Three other species might also be confused with *R. formosa*: *R. botrytis* has white branches tipped with pink; *R. holorubella* has reddish to red-brown branches without yellow tips and not bruising black; and *R. flava* has deep yellow branches, often with a pinkish tint.

Where and When—All species occur late summer to fall in woods, generally conifers. *R. flava* grows on rotted wood while the rest appear on the soil.

Nature of Toxin—Type III, gastrointestinal.

Sarcosphaera

Description—*Fruiting Body:* subterranean, large (up to 18 cm), fleshy, initially a white hollow smooth ball, later splitting in stellate manner to expose a purple hymenium; *Flesh:* white, fragile; *Underside:* white, tomentose.

Distinguishing Features—1) subterranean habit; 2) stellate splitting; and 3) purple hymenium.

Remarks—No other genus resembles this.

Name Derivation—*Sarcosphaera* means flesh ball.

Poisonous Species—One species, *S. eximia*, is poisonous. It grows as a hollow sphere 5-10 cm in diameter, later splitting in a star-like manner. Both outer and inner surface are white at first, but the inner turns deep violet.

Where and When—*S. eximia* appears spring and fall on soft or sandy soil, usually under conifers.

Nature of Toxin—Type III, gastrointestinal or possibly type Ib, *Gyromitra* toxin.

Mushroom Toxicology

Mushroom poisoning is not common in the United States and Canada because the collecting of wild mushrooms is not common. In Europe, however, collectors are numerous and eager to try almost any mushroom. In Poland, for example, as many as 59 deaths have been recorded in a single year. German collectors are even less lucky, with 200 fatal cases reported in one year.

R. Buck[1] reviewed the North American literature in 1964 and could report only 36 cases of fatalities, most of which were due to unidentified mushrooms. Of those reported, *Amanita verna* and *A. phalloides* were the most frequent causes; *Gyromitra esculenta*, *Amanita pantherina*, and *Psilocybe baeocystis* were also reported, causing four deaths.

Since mushroom poisoning is so rare in North America, most hospitals are poorly prepared for diagnosis of the poisoning and identification of the causal agent. It is also frustrating to have no central (public health) clearing agency for statistical information on mushroom poisoning. It has been estimated that as many as 50 deaths occur in North America each year, but most go unreported.

I The Deadly Toxins

Ia   The Deadly Delayed Syndrome

Chemistry of the cyclopeptide toxins: Toxins found in certain species of *Amanita, Galerina, Conocybe,* possible *Lepiota helveola* and others fit into the general cyclopeptide category. These compounds are further divided into the amatoxins and the phallotoxins. Both are composed of amino acids linked together in cyclic fashion, joined by a bridge of sulphur connecting the inner circle. Phalloidin can be differentiated into six compounds and amanitin consists of five or more compounds.

Not all cyclopeptide toxins are contained in each mushroom. The dangerous *Galerina* species for example contains only amatoxins and not phallotoxins. *Amanita rubescens* on the other hand

1. R. Buck, "Poisoning by Wild Mushrooms," *Clinical Medicine* 71:1964

contains only phallotoxins.

The rapid onset of this poisoning does not occur clinically when mushrooms containing cyclopeptides are ingested. The very distinctive delay of symptoms occurs when amatoxins (not phallotoxins) are injected interperitoneally in a laboratory animal. Because of this evidence it is now thought that amatoxins alone are the sole cause of the deadly delayed poisoning syndrome. It also explains why *A. rubescens* is safely eaten though it can hardly be recommended.

Both toxins, amanitin and phalloidin destroy liver function but in quite different ways. Phalloidin is known to disrupt the cell membrane but alpha-amanitin destroys the nucleolus of the cell and its RNA so that the essential DNA transcription and protein synthesis cannot occur. Another site of amanitin activity is the kidney. This damage is probably associated with liver destruction.

Symptoms. Six to twenty-four hours or as late as thirty hours after ingestion symptoms will appear (grave prognosis if symptoms are delayed beyond 12 hours).

These symptoms include severe abdominal cramps, nausea, vomiting, diarrhea (usually bloody), tender enlarged liver, anuria, oliguria, jaundice, pulmonary edema, headache, confusion, hypoglycemia, coma, and convulsions. Temporary recovery may occur, with a recurrence and worsening of symptoms on the third and fourth days. Death occurs in 34% to 63% of the cases, usually as a result of acute liver degeneration.

Treatment. There is no specific, proven antidote for poisoning by the cyclopeptide toxins. Emetics or lavage are generally futile because of the delay in expression of symptoms, but should be carried out if vomiting and diarrhea have not yet commenced. This should be followed by instillation of activated charcoal. Loss in blood pressure and collapse are due to loss in fluids, sugar, and sodium chloride; hence, fluid and electrolyte maintenance is important. Increase protein intake. Hemodialysis or peritoneal dialysis may be helpful. Oral administration of broad spectrum antibiotics may aid in minimizing liver damage. Cortisteroids administered first intravenously and later orally are believed to be of help in the later, critical phase. Additional treatment should be largely supportive and symptomatic. An antidote of chopped, raw rabbit brains and stomach has been recommended but has not been widely accepted. A serum, developed in France, has not been accepted either, since the cyclopeptide toxins are very rapidly bound to tissues and to serum albumen. Recently there have been several reported cases of treatment with thiotic (alpha lipoic) acid. A dose of 300 mg intravenously over twenty-four hours, repeated over several days, has significantly reduced the mortality rate in animals. Cytochrome C is most recently reported as an antidote. In combination with penicillin G, this chemical has increased survival in mice.

V.E. Tyler[2] presented a chromatographic technique for the detection of cyclopeptide toxins which is extremely useful should research into the nature of the toxin be necessary.

Ib   The Gyromitra Toxin

The poisons which occur sporadically in species of *Gyromitra*, and also possibly in *Morchella, Verpa* and probably many other ascomycetes such as *Sarcosphaera* are among the most severe of mushroom toxins.

Symptoms. Poisoning symptoms are similar to the deadly delayed syndrome. The latent period between the consumption of mushrooms is shorter, rarely less than 2 hours and commonly 6-8 hours. At this time a patient has a feeling of fullness of stomach followed by violent vomiting and diarrhea which may persist for one or two days. Headache, lassitude, cramps, and severe pain in the liver and gastric region are followed by jaundice. In severe cases the patient undergoes general collapse, the pulse becomes irregular, breathing is difficult, and delirium and convulsions occur; death may occur from heart failure or liver damage, usually within ten days.

2. V. E. Tyler, "Poisonous Mushrooms." *Progress in Chemical Toxicology*, ed. Abraham Stolman. (New York and London: Academic Press, 1963). I: pp. 345-346.

Mortality rates are generally around 2% to 4%. Poisoning of this nature is common in Europe, often involving large groups of people. Relatively few poisonings have occurred in the United States and Canada. It is disconcerting that some people do not get sick after eating this mushroom. The reason probably lies in the fact that the toxin, gyromitrin (a derivative of monomethylhydrazine) is water soluble and volatile, so that cooking uncovered in several changes of water can extract the poison. This method cannot be recommended as a universal detoxification technique since fatal cases are known with *G. esculenta* cooked with this method. Though in the western U.S. no poisonings from *Gyromitra esculenta* have been reported, poisonings are known for *G. infula* in the western area. Several authors mention that partially decomposed mushrooms are especially dangerous.

Treatment. Methods of treatment include: gastric lavage, administration of cathartics, enemas, and forced fluids. Additional care is largely symptomatic and supportive.

The Reif test may be employed to distinguish poisonous *Gyromitra* species from other edible morsels.

Extraction: 10 grams fresh tissue or 1 gram dried is chopped or ground and placed in a 500 ml. flask with 40 ml. water, 10 ml. of 10% sodium hydroxide, 5 grams of sodium chloride and a few glass beads. This solution is then attached to a condensor after mixing and allowed to heat carefully until 30 ml. of distillate are collected.

Colour Test: To 15 ml. of this distillate add 15 drops of 0.5% selenium in concentrated sulphuric acid. Warm on a steam table for 15 minutes. *Gyromitra* species produce a red precipitate of selenium. Tissues of *Morchella* do not produce this precipitate.

II Nervous System Toxins

IIa Toggle Switch Intoxication

Chemistry of the autonomic system affecting *Amanita* species: It has long been scientifically accepted that substances affecting the central nervous system occur in *A. muscaria* and its relatives. Muscarine, an alkaloid, was the first to be discovered in *A. mus-*

caria. Muscarine could be shown to have a direct effect on the central nervous system, and was erroneously thought to be the active agent in *A. muscaria* and *A. pantherina*. As late as 1970, we have found references to atropine therapy for *A. muscaria* poisoning. This is an incorrect treatment, since the total muscarine content is extremely low (0.0002% in fresh tissue), too low for physiological activity. Unfortunately, atropine exacerbates the toxic effects of another *Amanita* alkaloid, ibotenic acid. Thus we may speculate that atropine may have contributed to the scattered deaths attributed to this mushroom.

Other species of *Amanita*, like *A. citrina* and *A. porphyria*, have been reported to contain bufotenine (5-OH-N. N dimethyl tryptamine), which is central acting when administered intravenously, as well as the powerful hallucinogen DMT (N. N. dimethyl tryptamine). Their occurrence in these mushrooms is too low for physiological activity.

Now accepted as the principal active material in toggle-switch intoxication is ibotenic acid, ($C_5H_8N_2O_5$) an acidic, optically inactive, a-amino acid with a heterocyclic component. The name was derived from *Ibotengu-take*, the Japanese designation for *Amanita strobiliformis*. Since its first description, ibotenic acid has been reported in relatively few *Amanita* species. Since it is unstable, simple techniques for identification cannot be described in this book.

Two additional stereoisomers, muscimol and muscazone, are reported as occurring in these mushrooms. They are both centrally active, although muscazone considerably less so than muscimol.

Ibotenic acid transmutes quite easily into muscimole and muscizone with cooking, drying and laboratory extraction procedures. Because of this there is no way one can tell how much of each component is present in fresh, undisturbed mushrooms.

The concentration of ibotenic acid in mushroom tissue has been found to vary with the season. Summer mushrooms have been found to be more potent than autumn mushrooms. In addition, the highest concentration has been found to be in pigmented tissue under the skin. An average concentration of 70 mg/g fresh mushrooms (or 35 mg/g dried) is typical.

The pharmacological and psychological effects of muscimol and ibotenic acid have been discovered only in recent years. Neither drug evokes the typical hallucinogenic syndrome characteristic of LSD, psilocybin, or mescaline, and neither reproduces the exact symptoms of *A. muscaria* intoxication. Muscimol was found to be some five times more active than ibotenic acid, 7.5-10 mg taken orally was an active dose. Muscimol is quite toxic—LD_{50} [3] = 2.4 mg/kg for mice and 3.5 mg/kg for rats.

Toggle switch intoxication works much like an electrical switch which directs circuitry from one channel to another. When switched to the most common channel, the chemical affects the cerebellum and is characterized by hallucinations with minor muscle spasms. More rarely the primary site of activity is the medulla which is responsible for motor control. This variation is less likely to occur but when it does, the experience is an unpleasant one which resembles a long lasting epilectic fit.

Symptoms: After fifteen to thirty minutes the patient may become drowsy or fall asleep. This is followed by hallucinations, confusion or muscle spasms.

The psychoactive compounds in *A. muscaria* are probably not metabolized in the body. In various archaic societies, people were aware that the urine of intoxicated persons (and animals) was quite suitable for a "second-hand" kick.

As was mentioned, **atropine exacerbates the toxic effects of muscimol and ibotenic acid and should not be administered.** Recommendation of its use in older literature was based on the mistaken belief that muscarine was the principal toxin in *A. muscaria* and *A. pantherina*. Bear in mind that muscimol tends to increase the potency of sedatives and tranquillizers. Prognosis for

3. Amount of poison given to a population in which 50% of the recipients die.

recovery is high, although deaths are known. In Germany, where such poisonings are frequent, death rates of 5.5% and 1.54% are known for *A. muscaria* and *A. pantherina* respectively.

Treatment: Proper treatment involves removing the toxin through gastic lavage and emetics. This may be followed by chlorpromazine to terminate the hallucinations followed by stimulants such as coffee or tea if the patient becomes depressed. Other treatment is symptomatic.

Ethnobotanical significance: In recent years the use of *Amanita muscaria* as an intoxicant has been the basis of some interesting ethnobotanical research. In the past, most popular mushroom books have treated this mushroom (and *A. pantherina*) as either "deadly" or "poisonous". Actually, documented deaths from *A. muscaria* poisoning are rare or non-existent. Deaths from *A. pantherina* are known, however, both in the United States and Europe. The writings of R. Gordon Wasson and John Allegro have tended to open a credibility gap between the ethnobotanists and the mycophagists. On one hand, some say that the historical use of *A. muscaria* as a divine intoxicant had a directional influence on many eastern and western cultures, while on the other hand popular mushroom books written for pot-hunters treat this mushroom as strictly *verboten*.

R. Gordon Wasson's research into the relationship between mushrooms and culture started with a personal discovery. Wasson regarded himself as a **mycophobe**—that is, having a natural dislike or fear regarding fungi. On the other hand, his wife had a feeling for mushrooms which was more akin to affection—she was a **mycophile**. Discussions soon showed that the differences between them were cultural, not natural. Wasson's background was Anglo-Saxon, and his wife's Russian.

The Wassons stumbled onto an interesting and culturally distinctive feature which, of course, does not play any role of sociological importance in our culture, but which has played a basic role in some cultures. In fact, mushrooms played quite a significant role in some mycophillian cultures—even to the point of being included into religious practices.

Whatever the form of social or religious expression, in all cases, the mushrooms were ingested to produce some sort of intoxication. It must be pointed out that while "intoxication" also refers to alcoholic drunkeness, there is no comparison between the two phenomena. From all reports, mushroom intoxication can be described as a means to discover physical and psychological ecstasy—experiences which are not normally associated with being drunk.

Wasson's description[4] of the hallucinogenic properties of *A. muscaria* ("fly agaric") will perhaps illustrate this point.

a. It begins to act in fifteen or twenty minutes and the effects last for hours.

b. First it is a soporific. One goes to sleep for about two hours, and the sleep is not normal. One cannot be roused from it, but is sometimes aware of the sounds round about. In this half-sleep sometimes one has coloured visions that respond, at least to some extent, to one's desires.

c. Some subjects enjoy a feeling of elation that lasts for three or four hours after waking from the sleep. In this stage it is interesting to note the superiority of this drug over alcohol is particularly emphasized: the fly agaric is not merely better, it belongs to a different and superior order of inebriant, according to those who have enjoyed the experience. During this state the subject is often capable of extraordinary feats of physical effort, and enjoys performing them.

d. A peculiar feature of the fly agaric is that its hallucinogenic properties pass into the urine, and another may drink this urine to enjoy the same effect. Indeed it is said that the urine of three or four successive drinkers may be thus consumed without noticeable loss of inebriating effect. This surprising trait of fly agaric inebriation is unique in the hallucinogenic world, so far as our present knowledge goes.

4. R.G. Wasson, "Fly Agaric and Man," *Ethnopharmacological Search for Psychoactive Drugs*, ed. D.H. Efron. (Washington: U.S. Department of Health, Education and Welfare, 1967). Public Health Publication, 1645: pp. 412-173.

The soporific and kinetic effects of the fly amanita are utterly unlike anything produced by the mushrooms of the genus *Psilocybe* of Mexico.

In western society, the only culturally acceptable inebriant is alcohol. Yet there is nothing in the nature of alcohol that recommends this status. At low levels it is certainly a tongue loosener and whets the appetite, but heavy usage only brings about regret the morning after.

In light of this, we again must be careful not to equate the effects of mushrooms and alcohol. Mushroom experiences can be described in terms of ecstasy—an experience which cannot always be equated with pleasure.

One of the risks involved in hallucinogenic, mind-expanding experiences is instant psychoanalysis. To gain insight into one's mind is not always a pleasant experience.

Another risk of *A. muscaria* involves what I call toggle-switch intoxication, which in its rarer form causes uncontrolled muscular spasms historically regarded as closeness to God, but in terms of contemporary society this feature can hardly be considered desirable.

An *Amanita muscaria* culture is rapidly emerging, much like the LSD excursions of the early '60s. We have come across much folklore concerning the "safe" use of this mushroom, but so far all methods of preparation (peeling, cooking, etc.) only serve to extract or avoid the toxins. These treatments will not eliminate the chances of a muscular spasm episode.

This latter problem is the reason why we do not recommend the usage of *A. muscaria* or *A. pantherina*. Eating these mushrooms is akin to befriending a wolverine. There are times when it will let you stroke its soft fur and purr in return, but on another occasion it will run chattering teeth up and down your arm before you have a chance to scream.

A current common name of *A. muscaria* is the fly agaric. This is supposedly derived from the belief that the mushroom has insecticidal properties. Anyone who has prepared a milk and *muscaria* concoction soon discovers that the only flies which die in the mixture are those which inadvertently drown. More recently, it has been accepted that the fly epithet is more accurately associated with madness. Those suffering with mental disorders were considered to be seized by the "fly of divine possession".

In the second millenium before Christ, the Aryans swept down from the north through Afghanistan and occupied the valley of the Indus. All that we know of the Aryans comes to us from a collection of 1,028 hymns they composed after arriving in the Indus valley. This collection of psalms or verses is one of the four vedas, the sacred scriptures of Hinduism. The subsequent cuneiform records were not inscribed for a thousand years and more afterwards. The chief method for preserving these Vedic hymns was memory. Western scholars have recently transcribed the Rig Veda words and music from the mouths of Hindu priests. Translations from these texts have been available for 120 years but the meanings of certain passages were obscure, among them references to an intoxicating beverage called "soma", which until recent times was considered the alcoholic derivative of a wild herb.

R. Gordon Wasson and his collaborator, Wendy Doniger O'Flaherty, have gathered credible evidence that this beverage soma, which was praised in the Rig Vedic hymn, was *A. muscaria*. In an elaborate interpretation of every reference to soma, they have shown that this beverage could not have been derived from a plant other than a mushroom. The references to the form of the plant and its effects, even so far as the property of its being passed in the urine, all seem to indicate one mushroom—*A. muscaria*.

These links have been traced to contemporary Siberian tribes which all revere the birch (a tree which is frequently found in association with *A. muscaria*). To R. Gordon Wasson, "The birch is the Tree of Life . . . The *Axis Mundi*, the Pillar of Heaven, and the fly-agaric is the Marvellous Herb." If he is correct, he has integrated a cult of mushroom and tree that has reached from one side of Eurasia to the other, and from the present time to the distant reaches of the Stone Age. It is not difficult to accept Wasson's

104

thesis; however, it is more difficult to even understand John Allegro's thesis.

John Allegro, scholar of the Dead Sea scrolls, has presented an alternative theory to Christianity in his book, *The Sacred Mushroom and the Cross*. This theory, again based upon *Amanita muscaria*, leads the reader through all sorts of linguistic "equivalences" which culminate in the theory that Jesus = penis = mushroom. According to this master of the Sumerian language, the New Testament was not written because of Jesus Christ, but instead to be a codex for a persecuted mushroom and sex cult. As anything is possible, Allegro could ultimately prove to be right, but so far he has not had a single colleague step forward to support his theory, much in contrast to Wasson's work. Indeed, one colleague of Allegro stated if one accepts the Jesus = penis = mushroom, it is also necessary to consider a hospital (hos-spit-al) as a house where we all go to spit.

The literature is full of additional references to special mushrooms. It is the dominant and powerful mushroom in Slavic fairy tales. The most famous work referring to one of the mushroom's unsuspected properties is Lewis Carroll's *Alice in Wonderland*. Whether or not one actually knows what the mushroom is, one has undoubtedly read of its effects on little Alice:

Then it got off the mushroom and crawled away into the grass merely remarking as it went, "One side will make you taller and the other side will make you grow shorter."

One side of what, the other side of what? thought Alice to herself.

"Of the mushroom," said the caterpillar, just as if she had asked aloud; and in another moment it was out of sight.

IIb Sweat Producing Muscarine Poisoning

This autonomic nervous system poison is unfortunately named. It was first recognized in *Amanita muscaria* but, according to recent research, is found in concentration too low for physiological activity. Muscarine is more characteristically found in species of *Inocybe* and *Clitocybe*. The concentration of muscarine in some species is amazingly high. A danger is that with many people currently seeking "magic" mushrooms, there is a chance that some unfortunate soul might make a fatal mistake with these harmless-appearing brown mushrooms.

The lethal dose of muscarine taken orally varies for an adult person, but ranges between 0.3 and 0.5 grams. Since species vary in actual muscarine content, the lethal dosage of fresh mushrooms will range between 20-1000 grams, sometimes more.

Symptoms. Muscarine poisoning is quite distinctive due to the perspiring intoxication caused by a strong irritation of the parasympathetic nervous system. The symptoms appear within 15 to 30 minutes following ingestion.

These symptoms involve: strong excretion of sweat, salivation, secretions of the nose, bronchi, and pancreatic glands, increase in intestinal movements, vomiting, diarrhea, stomach ache, slowing down of heart functions, peripheral vasodilation especially in the head, lowering of blood pressure, extremities growing cold, and a tendency to collapse.

The symptoms are accompanied by a disturbance of eyesight and breathing difficulties. The rare occurrence of death is due to these breathing difficulties and weakening of the heart muscles.

Treatment. Muscarine poisoning is perhaps the easiest to treat. Sudden reversal of symptoms can be brought about by hypodermic administration of atropine sulphate 0.5 - 1.0 mg repeated in one half hour if necessary. After vomiting has ceased, dilute saline solutions and glucose should be administered orally in large amounts.

A chromatographic technique for the detection of muscarine has been presented by Tyler[5].

5. V.E. Tyler, "Poisonous Mushrooms," *Progress in Chemical Toxicology*, ed. Abraham Stolman. (New York and London: Academic Press, 1963), Vol. 1, p. 351.

IIc   Teonanacatl

Chemistry of species containing psilocybin/psilocin: Mushrooms which contain psilocybin/psilocin are difficult to consider poisonous. They must, however, be treated with the utmost respect since the user is dealing with a powerful mind-altering drug. This is an experience which an individual will not necessarily relish. In addition, a child's death has been attributed to an overdose of *Psilocybe baeocystis*.

Young children have been observed to be more susceptible to psilocybin/psilocin. The prolonged clinical course in some intoxicated children differs dramatically from adults.

The psychotomimetic effects of mescaline, LSD, and psilocybin/psilocin are similar. The duration of psilocybin and psilocin intoxication is shorter than for either LSD or mescaline. The dosage for psilocybin/psilocin is 6-20 mg. LSD is 120-150 times more powerful, and mescaline about an order of magnitude less potent. Evidence of cross tolerance among the three drugs indicates that their psychic effect is due to the same mechanism of action in the brain. Overall, psilocybin tends to inhibit the parasympathetic hormone serotonin.

Psilocybin intoxication: Following the ingestion of psilocybin-containing mushrooms, psychotomimetic symptoms resembling those induced by lysergic acid diethylamide (LSD) commence in about 30-60 minutes and continue for several hours. The patient may display anxiety and difficulty in concentration and understanding. Changes in sensory perception, including sensitivity to touch and distortion of tactile sensations, as well as changes in size, shape, colour, and depth of vision with kaleidoscopic variations, are noted. The mood is altered: usually it is elevated, but depression may occur. Both elementary hallucinations, such as the appearance of coloured lights and patterns on closing the eyes, and true hallucinations may be experienced.

Special attention should be given to cases of children who have ingested these mushrooms. They may develop fever to

106°F and demonstrate clonic-tonic convulsions. Both of these symptoms may be life threatening.

Treatment. Persons suffering from this type of mushroom poisoning ordinarily recover spontaneously and completely in 5-10 hours. Gastric lavage or emetics may hasten recovery; other treatment is symptomatic.

We have observed many hospital emergency room cases of psilocybin mushroom poisoning. In most cases the patient had collected the mushrooms, ate them purposely "to get high" and became fearful that the mushrooms were misidentified. The results were intense anxiety with the conviction they were going to die. In one case we were able to positively identify the mushrooms as *Psilocybe semilanceata* and instantly reverse these effects simply by informing the patient.

There is no field test for psilocybin/psilocin. Enos, in *Key to the North American Psilocybin Mushroom,* popularized a field colour test using the photographic chemical metol (p-methylaminophenol sulphate). This test clearly does not work since metol and a similar chemical used in paper chromatography (p-dimethylaminobenzaldehyde) are not specific and are a substrate for certain phenol oxidases which are widely distributed. The edible mushroom *Agaricus bisporus* for example reacts 'positive' in terms of this reported field test.

There is a simple chromatographic test[6] for psilocybin and psilocin which we outline here:

Extraction: Grind several mushrooms in a small quantity of cold methanol. Let settle and alternately shake for 30 minutes.

Chromatography: Take a 20 cm circular piece of Whatman #1 filter paper and fit over the inner lid of a 15 cm petri dish. Cut a paper tongue in the centre approximately 1 cm x 4 cm, so that the tongue will drop down to the solvent at the bottom of the dish. The supernatent fluid is then spotted at

6. Modified from V.E. Tyler, "Poisonous Mushrooms," *Progress in Chemical Toxicology,* ed. Abraham Stolman. (New York and London: Academic Press, 1963). Vol. 1, p. 351.

the point of attachment of the "tongue", being careful to keep the zone of spotting smaller than 2-3 mm. A micropipette and hair dryer would be desirable here.

Resolution: of psilocybin and psilocin is carried out with water saturated *n* butanol for 2 hours, or until the solvent front reaches the edge of the dish. At this point remove the sheet from the dish and air dry. Spray with a mixture of *p*-dimethylaminobenzaldehyde which has been first dissolved in a minute amount of alcohol, then with 1 N hydrochloric acid.

On drying in warm air, psilocybin should appear as a reddish zone (R_f 0.25), and psilocin a blue-violet zone (R_f 0.53).

Ethnobotanical significance: Teonanacatl, which means flesh of the gods in Aztec, is only one of the many drugs used by Shamans (curandero) in Mexico's Oaxaca State. These mushrooms, comprised of a number of *Psilocybe* and *Conocybe* species, are incorporated to this day into magic and religious ceremonies. This usage of these mushrooms as a divinatory substance can be traced back at least 3000 years. In Guatamala, stones have been found in the form of mushroom caps with a spirit figure on the stems.

The Spanish chroniclers and naturalists who first came to the New World mentioned several plants which were stimulating, narcotic, or intoxicating. The use of these plants in religious ceremonies was frowned upon by the early missionaries and, indeed, mushrooms were thought to be agents of the devil. The natives, however, continued secretly to use these drugs which they considered to be holy, even after they were converted to Christianity.

As early as 1936, some North American investigators established that mushrooms were still being used in religious ceremonies in certain areas of southern Mexico. In the summer of 1955, R. Gordon Wasson, V. P. Wasson, and French mycologist Roger Heim, were the first white persons to attend the once secret mushroom ceremony. Dr Heim was able to identify the mushrooms as species of *Psilocybe* and *Panaeolus*. Later, Albert Hofmann at Sandoz Laboratories in Switzerland, discovered the chemical identity and synthesis of psilocybin/psilocin.

R. Gordon Wasson popularized the magic mushrooms of

Mexico in a now classic issue of *Life* magazine and in prolific subsequent writings. It is almost as though he were a reincarnation of an Aztec priest watching his ancient culture rise again from its ashes like the phoenix. Today the use of intoxicating mushrooms has spread from the state of Oaxaca to the entire world, as people discover magic mushrooms growing at their very feet. We can do nothing at this time to prevent people from using these mushrooms, but perhaps we can suggest how to use them and, above all, to respect them.

In the Mexican ceremony, the mushrooms speak through the curandero, almost as though he or she is not present. The nocturnal meeting, chosen because the darkness tends to accentuate unfamiliar shapes and textures, is a form of group psychotherapy. In these meetings the mushroom spirit is asked to answer questions about a sick person, a missing goat, or stolen money. It seems significant that these people sincerely believe in these visions. A friend who personally observed one such ceremony was surprised to discover the missing goat exactly where the mushroom directed the shaman to tell the owner.

The group therapy approach and environment surrounding the use of the drug plant are very similar to the use of the jungle vine *Banisteriopsis*, in Peru as described by Marlena del Rios in *The Visionary Vine*.

Carlos Castaneda, in books about his acquantance with don Juan, tells us about the use of *Psilocybe* species, *Datura* species, and peyote in northern Mexico. These plants are manifested in the form of allies which perform through the user or shaman. Don Juan used the mushroom much like a snuff in a smoking mixture. Through Castaneda's lucid descriptions, the mushroom experiences are seen to be powerful, bringing about a re-evaluation of life's goals, and other deep explorations of the mind. He has been criticized by scholars because he has refused to produce don Juan for public view, but this seems to be the older sorcerer's way. Some have said that don Juan is fictitious, but it does not matter to me if he is "real" or a composite of several personalities. What

110

does matter is that the books transcend other ethnobotanical explorations of drug uses in exotic cultures, and show amazing parallels with eastern religions and even modern psychotherapy techniques.

Albert Hofmann and fellow Swiss workers at Sandoz Laboratories first received some specimens of cultivated *Psilocybe mexicana* from Roger Heim in 1956. At this time they tried to demonstrate the psychotomimetic properties of this mushroom in experimental animals. The results were frustrating and inconclusive. Faced with the risk of exhausting their limited supply, Hofmann ingested, under strict observation, a large quantity of mushrooms. His reaction[7] follows:

Thirty minutes after taking the mushrooms the exterior world began to undergo a strange transformation. Everything assumed a Mexican character. As I was perfectly well aware that my knowledge of the Mexican origin of the mushroom would lead me to imagine only Mexican scenery, I tried deliberately to look on my environment as I knew it normally. But all voluntary efforts to look at things in their customary forms and colours proved ineffective. Whether my eyes were closed or open I saw only Mexican motifs and colours. When the doctor supervising the experiment bent over me to check my blood pressure, he was transformed into an Aztec priest and I would not have been astonished if he had drawn an obsidian knife. In spite of the seriousness of the situation, it amused me to see how the Germanic face of my colleagues had acquired a purely Indian expression. At the peak of the intoxication, about 1½ hours after ingestion of the mushrooms, the rush of interior pictures, mostly abstract motifs rapidly changing in shape and colour, reached such an alarming degree that I feared that I would be torn into this whirlpool of form and colour and would dissolve. After about six hours the dream came to an end. Subjectively, I had no idea how long this condition had lasted. I felt my return to everyday reality to be a happy return from a strange, fantastic but quite really experienced world into an old and familiar home.

7. A. Hofmann, "The Discovery of LSD and Subsequent Investigations on Naturally Occurring Hallucinogens", *Discoveries in Biological Psychiatry*. (Philadelphia: Lippincott), p. 98.

At this point it seems necessary to record some of my own experiences with magic mushrooms.[8] In 1967, when I came to the Northwest region of the U.S.A., I knew a great deal about both edible and poisonous mushrooms, but I did not have much concern about the little brown ones. When people began to inquire about hallucinogenic mushrooms, I attempted to learn about them in order to prevent people from poisoning themselves. My policy at that time was (and still is) not to encourage or endorse the use of these magic mushrooms but to try to identify any mushroom (poisonous, edible, or hallucinogenic) brought into my class or office. Until 1969 we did not identify a single magic mushroom for a hopeful mushroom seeker. In 1969, Jeff Fine, a graduate student, began his studies on the Northwestern species of *Naematoloma, Stropharia* and *Psilocybe*. We discovered five species of psilocybin mushrooms in abundance.

During the course of his thesis research, I decided to try these psychedelic mushrooms at least for the sake of maintaining objectivity when discussing contemporary drug use problems in my general biology class. We had many discussions beforehand about what other people experienced with mushrooms, mainly because I was strictly a neophyte and was eager to enter the experience but wanted to see through the doors before I went in. One point which Jeff brought up, which later turned out to be very valid, was that LSD gave visual patterns and images, but that psilocybin allowed you to sit down and talk with your hallucinations.

When the mushrooms began to appear in the fall of 1969. We first tried very low levels of *P. semilanceata* and *P. stuntzii* to test our tolerance.

Later we tried a larger dose of *P. stuntzii*, experiencing visual distortion, colour changes, and accentuation of patterns much like an LSD or mescaline experience. One interesting effect of the mushroom was that my mind was able to alter the perceptual image of a person into the kind of person I perceived him or her to

8. The experiences described are those of Dr. Richard Haard.

112

be (e.g., a devilish person grew horns and tail). Thus far I have tried six species and have noticed very decisive differences amongst them. *P. stuntzii* generally lets me look into the order which my inner mind forces on the rest of me; *P. semilanceata* is a model builder allowing me to look into the past, present, and future of my life and activities, even into the very nature of life and eternity; *P. strictipes* and *P. baeocystis* both give a visual adventure, with *baeocystis* the most visual mushroom thus far experienced.

About this point in my explorations I became very flippant about my use of these intoxicants. I began to slip into a mode of using the mushrooms as an inebriant in the Western fashion, rather than with a distinct goal in mind. To do this is to give the mushroom "ally" a free hand, and this is most dangerous. One evening I ate twenty dried specimens of *P. semilanceata*, normally a minimal dose for this weak mushroom. Much to my surprise and occasional dismay, I was pulled into the heaviest psychic experience I have ever encountered. I was possessed by the mushroom spirit almost as if it sought to teach me a lesson. It now seems that I was drawn into a psychoanalysis which allowed me to act out my personal conflicts by alternately becoming the conflicting selves and always observing myself at the same time. Something had suddenly appeared out of the creative depths of my mind, something of which I was previously unaware. I underwent an awesome, fear-filled, but enlightening experience. Without respect you may be pulled into a vortex which you have no desire to enter.

If you insist on stepping through the door of ecstasy, then prepare yourself with the writing of such people as John Lilly and Carlos Castenada.[9] These experiences should be reserved as a special occasion in your life, with many months or even years spent in preparation for the potential experience. Remember, Aldous Huxley used LSD and psilocybin only 12 times *in his life*.

9. See recommended reading at the rear of this book.

III   The Gastrointestinal Irritants

The most common type of poisoning we have encountered is gastrointestinal. Many species are involved, some of which are very dangerous—others give a temporary discomfort which is indistinguishable from the stomach flu. We wish to emphasize that the poisonous mushrooms lumped into this catchall category have toxins that are largely unknown. Poisoning from the deadly toxins also includes gastric upset along with liver and kidney damage.

Some species are considered quite dangerous. *Rhodophyllus sinuatus* causes some kidney damage, and this property may extend to other mushrooms. *Lactarius torminosus* and *Tricholoma pardinum* are especially noteworthy for their severe gastrointestinal effects. Some species of *Russula* and *Lactarius*, and *Paxillus involutus* are toxic if eaten raw.

I poisoned myself on one occasion by tasting *Lactarius scrobiculatus* to see if it was acrid. It was, and a numbness spread down my throat which lasted about an hour. *Verpa bohemica* is especially troublesome, since about 1 in 200 mycophagists develop an allergy to the mushroom.

More frustrating, some mushrooms are good and perfectly edible to some, but quite indigestible to others. If we listed every mushroom which has caused gastrointestinal upset in the latter category, it would probably include every "edible" mushroom species.

Symptoms. Ingestion of mushrooms in this category generally induces typical gastrointestinal upset in a few hours. The symptoms include nausea, vomiting, and diarrhea in a wide range of degrees of severity. Abdominal cramps and intense pain may be included. In most cases the symptoms terminate spontaneously in a few hours, and the patient returns to normal in a day or two.

Treatment. Remove the toxic material (if necessary!) and follow by symptomatic treatment with bed rest and a light diet.

The causal agents are varied. In some cases it is a definite toxin, characteristic for that species; in others it more closely resembles *Staphylococcus* food poisoning from eating spoiled mushrooms. Of special note is a chemical—nor-caperotic acid—which occurs in *Gomphus floccosus*. This mushroom occasionally causes heartburn, but the chemical nor-caperotic acid fed to rats over extended periods has also been found to enlarge their livers.

IV *Coprinus atramentarius*—Alcohol Toxicity

Here we have an odd sort of toxicity where the mushroom (*Coprinus atramentarius*) is only toxic when taken with alcohol, not necessarily in the same meal. The causal agent in this mushroom, now identified as coprine (N^5-(1-hydroxy-cyclopropy 1)-L-glutamine), acts like disulphiram, a chemical also used to cure alcoholism under the name Antabuse. The normal oxidation of alcohol in the blood is upset and accumulations of toxic acetaldehydes result.

Symptoms. Frequently sporadic symptoms include profound reddening of the face and neck, metallic taste in the mouth, numbness of extremities, palpitation and tachycardia, and a feeling of swelling of the hands. Nausea and vomiting are noted in some cases.

Treatment: Largely supportive as little can be done until the symptoms recede.

TABLE 1—Synopsis of Poisoning Symptoms & Treatment

Type		Symptoms	
Ia	6-24 hrs p. 95	Severe abdominal cramps, nausea, vomiting, diarrhea (usually bloody), tender enlarged liver, anuria, oliguria, jaundice, pulmonary edema, headache, confusion, hypoglycemia, coma, and convulsions; temporary recovery may occur, with worsening of symptoms on 3rd and 4th days.	Amanita cyclopeptide toxins
Ib	2-6 hrs p. 97	Fullness of stomach, followed by violent vomiting and diarrhea, headache, lassitude, cramps, severe pain in liver and gastric regions, jaundice; severe cases with general collapse, irregular pulse, difficult breathing, delirium, and convulsions.	
IIa	20 min.- 2 hrs p. 98	Narcosis, excitement, delirium, salivation, wheezing, diarrhea, slow pulse, dilated or constricted pupils, lacrimation, miosis, convulsions may or may not occur, hallucinations.	Ibotenic acid, muscimole
IIb	Minutes- 2 hrs. p. 106	Nausea, vomiting, diarrhea, profuse perspiration, secretions of nose, bronchi and pancreatic glands, circulatory failure, peripheral vasodilation especially in the head, cold extremities, disturbance in eyesight, and breathing difficulties.	Muscarine
IIc	30-60 min. p. 107	Psychotomimetic symptoms similar to those induced by LSD.	Psilocybin, Psilocin, Baeocystin
III	30-120 min. p. 114	Nausea, vomiting, diarrhea in a wide variety of degrees, sometimes with severe abdominal cramps and pain.	Varied, sometimes individual allergic reaction
IV	Minutes to 24 hrs. p. 116	Profound reddening, metallic taste in mouth, numbness of extremities, palpitation, tachycardia, feeling of swelling of hands, sometimes nausea and vomiting.	Disulphiram-like alcohol reaction (antabuse)

116

TABLE 1—*Continued*

Causal Organisms	Organs Affected	Treatment
Amanita verna, A. bisporigera, Galerina autumnalis, G. venenata, Lepiota helveola, Conocybe, others; see text, pp. 44, 46, 61, 71	Liver, kidney	No specific proven antidote; treatment mainly supportive and symptomatic; may include electrolyte maintenance, increased protein intake, hemodialysis, peritoneal dialysis, antibiotics or cortisteroids.
Gyromitra spp. Possibly *Verpa, Morchella, Sarcosphaera* and others; see text, pp. 86, 89, 94	Heart, liver, blood	Gastric lavage, administration of cathartics, enemas, and forced fluids, and other supportive and symptomatic treatment.
Amanita muscaria, A. pantherina, and others; see text, p. 46	Central nervous system	Gastric lavage or emetics; symptomatic treatment which may include chloropromazine to terminate hallucinations and stimulants such as tea or coffee.
Clitocybe dealbata, Inocybe, and others; not *Amanita muscaria, A. pantherina*; see text, pp. 34, 67	Autonomic nervous system	Hypodermic administration of atropine sulphate; oral solutions of saline and glucose.
Psilocybe sp., Stropharia spp., Conocybe spp., Panaeolus sp., Gymnopilus spectabilis; see text, pp. 71, 73, 74, 82	Central nervous system	Gastric lavage, emetics and possibly symptomatic treatment.
Varied and diverse.	Gastrointestinal, some evidence of hepatotoxin in *Rhodophyllus sp.*	Gastric lavage and emetics if necessary, symptomatic treatment, bed rest and light diet.
Coprinus atramentarius; see text, p. 79	Circulatory	Recovery usually spontaneous; in severe cases symptomatic treatment.

117

Glossary

Abrupt: terminates suddenly.

Acute: less than a right angle.

Adnate: entire width of gills attached to stem.

Adnexed: gill width tapering toward stem giving a narrow attachment.

Amygdaliform: almond shaped.

Amyloid: turning blueblack in Meltzer's.

Anastomose: to connect crosswise forming angular areas.

Angular: (of spores) not regular in outline.

Annulus: ring of tissue left on the stem from the torn partial veil; collar.

Antidote: neutralizing substance.

Anuria: urinary suppression or kidney failure.

Apex: summit, point farthest from the base.

Appendiculate: (of cap margin) hung with veil fragments.

Appressed: closely flattened down.

Ascendant: slanting upward.

Asci: reproductive cell of the Ascomycetes which contains the spores.

Ascomycete: fungi in which spores are borne in saclike cells called asci.

Atropine: salt of an alkaloid obtained from belladonna.

Autodeliquescent: becoming liquid by the process of autodigestion.

Basidia: cells in which meiosis occurs followed by the budding off of sexual spores.

Bilateral: (gill trama) hyphae diverge from a centre line and form a zone of more or less parallel hyphae on either side.

Bulbous: enlarged at base.

Caespitose: crowded close together but not attached.

Calyptra: cap, hood.

Calyptrate: bearing a cap or hood.

Campanulate: bell shaped.

Cap: pileus, top part of mushroom which bears fertile portion.

Carminophilous: staining in the aniline dye Carmine red.

Carpophore: cap, stem, and gills.

Cartilaginous: (consistency of tissue) tough but breaking with a snap.

Cathartic: purgative.

Caulocystidium: a cystidium-like cell on the stem.

Cellular: made of a thin layer of single protoplasmic units called cells.

Cheilocystidium: a cystidium on the edge of a gill.

Chromatogram: a record produced by chemical analysis by which a mixture of substances is separated by fractional extraction.

Chrysocystidium: a claviform structure usually with yellow contents when mounted in KOH.

Clamp connections: a small hollow semicircular protuberance that attaches to the wall of two adjoining cells arching over the septum.

Clavate: club-shaped.

Clitocyboid: species with subdecurrent gills and cap depressed in the centre.

Cobwebby: composed of threads as fine as a cobweb.

Collybioid: flesh of cap thin, cap flat to bell shaped and stem thin.

Coma: abnormal deep stupor.

Conchate: shaped like a shell.

Concolourous: same colour as.

Confluent: continuous.

Consistency: firmness of tissues.

Context: (cap) inner body tissue, flesh.

Convergent: hyphae of gill trama curve toward a median line.

Convex: (cap) regularly rounded; broadly obtuse.

Convoluted: folded like a brain.

Convulsions: involuntary muscle contractions and relaxations.

Coralloid: having the form of coral.

Cortina: a cobwebby type veil.

Cortinate: with a cortina.

Costate: ridged, fluted.

Crenate: scalloped.

Crenulate: very finely scalloped.

Crumbly: falling apart.

Cup-shaped: shaped like a cup.

Cuspinate: with a sharp point.

Cuticle: (cap or stem) a single surface layer

of differentiated tissue.

Cylindric: a shape having the same diameter throughout and flat ends, tube-like.

Cystidium: a large sterile cell situated between the basidia or behind them.

Decarboxilated: the process by which a substance loses a carboxyl radical such as carbon dioxide.

Decurrent: (gills) running down stem.

Depressed: (cap) central portion lower than the margin.

Dextrinoid: turning red in Meltzer's.

Dialysis: the passage of a solute through a membrane.

Dichotomous: forking in pairs.

Dimidiate: semicircular in outline.

Divergent: (gill trama) hyphae turning out from centre line.

Eccentric: (stem) off centre.

Echinulate: covered with small pointed spines.

Electrolyte: a solution which is a conductor of electricity.

Ellipsoid: football shaped.

Emarginate: notched near the stem.

Emetic: medicine that induces vomiting.

Epicutis: the outer layer of the cutis.

Epigeous: above ground.

Evanescent: only slightly developed and soon disappearing.

Exacerbate: increase severity.

Fibrillose: (cap or stem surface) having thin threadlike filaments which are more or less parallel.

Fibrous: composed of toughish stringlike material.

Filaments: fine threads.

Fimbriate: fringed with cystidia or finely torn.

Flabelliform: fan-shaped.

Flaring: (annulus) spreading away from the stem at its free margin.

Floccose: loose cottony, tufted.

Flocculent: minutely woolly.

Flora: the plants of a particular region.

Free: (gills) not attached to stem.

Free: (volva) not adhering to the stem.

Fructification: the fruiting body.

Fungi: a group of organisms generally considered to be plants but lacking chlorophyll.

Furfuraceous: covered with loose mealy substance.

Fuscous: smoky drab in colour.

Fusiform: spindle-shaped, tapering at both ends.

Gastrointestinal: pertaining to stomach or intestine.

Gastroenteritis: inflammation of stomach or intestine.

Gelatinous: jellylike.

Genus: a term of classification, each genus including related species.

Germ pore: a passageway in the spore wall through which a germ tube may pass.

Gills: the blade-like structures on the underside of the cap, fertile portion, lamellae.

Glabrous: smooth, without scales or hairs.

Glandular dots: pigmented dots which frequently smear due to glandular secretions.

Globose: spherical.

Glutinous: (cap) surface covered with a heavy layer of sticky material made up of dissolved gelatinous hyphae.

Habit: characteristic appearance or manner of growth.

Habitat: the natural place of growth.

Hemodialysis: removal of a chemical substance from the blood by passing the blood through semipermeable membranes bathed in select fluids.

Hemolysis: destruction of red blood cells with the diffusion of hemoglobin into the surrounding fluid.

Hepatic: pertaining to the liver.

Hepatotoxin: a cytotoxin specific for liver cells.

Heterocyclic: pertaining to ring compounds that contain other atoms in addition to carbon in the ring.

Hirsute: covered with long stiff hairs.

Hispid: covered with stiff bristle-like hairs usually visible to the naked eye.

Hyaline: clear and colourless.

Hygrophanous: watery in appearance; fades

as it dries.

Hymeniform: made of erect, usually claviform or pyriform, cells arranged in a palisade.

Hymenium: fertile portion.

Hymenophore: the entire fructification.

Hyphae: fungi filaments.

Hypodermium: inner layer of the epidermis or skin of a body.

Incised: as if cut into.

Inferior: (annulus) on lower part of stem.

Infundibuliform: funnel-shaped.

Inrolled: (margin) curled inward in a roll.

Interwoven: (gill trama) hyphae intermingled.

Intravenously: into a vein.

Inverse: hyphae turn inward to a median line.

Involute: rolled in.

Kinetic: pertaining to motion.

Lacerate: appearing as if torn.

Laciniate: slashed into lobes or coarsely cut.

Lamellae: a vertical plate on the lower surface of the cap; gills.

Lamellulae: a short gill not reaching the stem.

Lassitude: weariness, exhaustion.

Lateral: (stem) attached to one side of the cap.

Latex: juice from mushrooms of the genus *Lactarius*.

Lavage: washing out a cavity.

Lentiform: lens shaped.

Lethal: that which causes death.

Lignicolous: growing on wood.

Luminescent: an emission of light from living organisms.

Mammiform: conical with rounded apex.

Margin: edge.

Mealy: flecked, as with meal.

Membranous: thin and pliant like a membrane.

Mucilaginous: sticky.

Mycelium: a mass of fungal filaments or hyphae.

Mycenoid: cap bell-shaped to campanulate, flesh thin, margin straight.

Necrosis: death of areas of tissue.

Nodular: having small knots.

Oblong: longer than broad with sides nearly parallel.

Ochre: buff-coloured.

Ochraceus: ochre-yellow.

Oliguria: lowered amount of urine formation.

Ovoid: egg-shaped.

Palisade: an arrangement of elongated perpendicular cells in close proximity.

Palpitation: rapid or violent pulsation.

Papillae: a small nipple-shaped elevation.

Papillate: having one or more papillae.

Parallel: lines having the same direction and always staying the same distance apart.

Parasympathetic: pertaining to the craniosacral division of the autonomic nervous system.

Pellicle: a viscid or glutinous layer on the cap that easily peels.

Pendulous: hanging.

Peritoneal: concerning the membrane over the viscera and lining the abdominal cavity.

Persistent: retaining its place, shape or structure; not disappearing.

Petaloid: shaped like the petals of flowers.

Pileus: cap or structure that bears the hymenophore on its lower side.

Plage: smooth place near the appendix of a spore.

Plane: having a flat surface.

Pleurocystidium: cystidium occurring on the face of a gill.

Pleurotoid: species having lignicolous habit, attached gills, stem eccentric, lateral or lacking and continuous with cap.

Plicate: folded like a fan.

Pluteoid: fleshy mushroom with free gills and no volva or annulus.

Pores: small openings, the mouth of a tube.

Porose: possessing pores.

Protoplasmic: of the living and semifluid substance of cells.

Pruinose: finely powdered.

Pseudorhiza: a root-like extension of the stem.

Psychotomimetic: a hallucinogen producing illusions.

Pubescent: hairy.

Pulmonary edema: condition where lungs retain fluid.

Punctate: marked with small dots, points, scales, spots or hollows.

Radiately: spreading out from around a common centre.

Radicating: having a root-like extension.

Recurved: curved backward or downward.

Regular: (trama) parallel hyphae.

Reniform: kidney shaped.

Resupinate: fruiting structure lies on the substratum and faces outward.

Reticulate: netlike marks made by lines, veins or ridges which cross one another.

Revolute: rolled back or up.

Rhizomorph: a visible strand composed of mycelial filaments which attach to the substratum.

Rimose-areolate: cracked in such a way as to mark the surface in patches.

Ring: annulus.

Rugose: coarsely wrinkled.

Saccate: sac-like.

Scabrous: rough with short projections.

Sclerotium: arresting body of variable size composed of a hardened mass of hyphae, usually with a darkened rind from which fruiting bodies may develop.

Seceding: (gills) at first adnexed or adnate but later separating from the stem.

Septum: partition.

Serotonin: 5-Hydroxytrytamine, vasoconstrictor.

Serrate: notched like a saw.

Serrulate: minutely toothed.

Sessile: without a stem; absent.

Silky: composed of shiny, smooth, close-fitting fibrils.

Sinuate: (gills) having a concave indentation next to stem.

Soporific: inducing sleep.

Sordid: dirty or dingy colour.

Spatulate: spatula shaped.

Species: a group of individuals alike in a particular distinct genetic character.

Sphaerocysts: bloated hyphal cells originally 2-nucleate which fill with sap and in which the nuclei break into fragments.

Spiny stellate: having pointed protuberances in star pattern.

Spore: asexual reproductive body in fungi, usually of one or more cells surrounded by a thick wall.

Spore print: the spore mass obtained by placing the cap on a piece of paper.

Squamose: covered with scales.

Squamulose: covered with minute scales.

Stellately: star shaped.

Stem: stalk, ascending axis of organism growing away from point of attachment.

Sterile: not producing spores.

Stipe: stem.

Stipitate: having a stem.

Striate: having radiating furrows or lines on cap margin.

Strigose: having long, coarse, stiff hairs that are more or less appressed.

Stropharioid: a mushroom with purple spores, convex cap, attached gills and ring.

Subbulbous: somewhat bulbous.

Subcutis: layer of the cutis below the epicutis.

Subdecurrent: (gills) gill attachment extending only slightly down the stem.

Subfree: almost free.

Subglobose: almost spherical.

Subhymenium: a differentiated tissue which gives rise to the hymenium.

Subpruinose: slightly powdered.

Subradicating: slight prolongation of stem.

Substipitate: with a very short stem.

Substrate: the material on which a fungus grows.

Subterranean: underground.

Subtomentose: more or less woolly.

Sulcate: grooved.

Superior: (annulus) positioned on the upper part of the stem.

Surface: outer face, or outside.

Syndrome: a complex of symptoms.

Tachycardia: abnormal rapidity of heart action.

Terrestrial: growing on ground.

Tomentose: densely woolly.

Tomentum: hairy.

Toxin: poison.

Trama: the flesh or context of the cap or lamellae.

Translucent: capable of transmitting light without being transparent.

Tricholomoid: fleshy species with gills more or less sinuate.

Truncate: ending abruptly as if cut off.

Tuberculate: covered with small swellings.

Tubes: hollow cylinders of polypores and boletes that bear the hymenium.

Umbilicate: (cap) having a central depression.

Umbo: a raised conical mound on the centre of the cap.

Umbonate: (cap) with a raised knob in the centre.

Unguloid: hoof-shaped.

Universal veil: enveloping tissue which initially encloses fruiting body.

Ventricose: enlarged in the middle.

Verrucose: covered with small rounded warts.

Villose: with long weak hairs.

Vinaceous: pinkish.

Viscid: sticky, slippery.

Volva: remains of universal veil at base of stem.

Warty: covered with small rounded knots.

Zonate: marked with concentric bands of colour.

Bibliography

Taxonomy and Morphology

Ainsworth, G.C. and Sussman, A.S. editors, *The Fungi*. New York: Academic Press, 1966.

Alexoupolus, C.J. *Introductory Mycology*. New York: Wiley Press, 1970.

Dennis, R.W.G. *British Ascomycetes*. Lehre: J. Cramer, 1968.

Fine, J.L. "The Stropharioidae of Western Washington". Master's thesis, Western Washington State College, 1972.

Graham, V.O. *Mushrooms of the Great Lakes Region*. New York: Dover Publications, 1970.

Groves, J.W. *Edible and Poisonous Mushrooms of Canada*. Ottawa: Canada Dept. of Agriculture, 1962.

Ingold, C.T. *The Biology of Fungi*. rev. ed., London: Hutchinson Educational, 1973.

McKenny, M. and Stuntz, D. *The Savory Wild Mushroom*. 2nd ed., rev., Seattle and London: Univ. of Washington Press, 1971.

Nakamura, N. "A Survey of Amanita in Western Washington". Master's thesis, Univ. of Washington, 1965.

Peterson, R. editor, *Evolution in the Higher Basidiomycetes*. Knoxville: Univ. of Tennessee, 1971.

Robinson, R.K. *Ecology of Fungi*. London: English Univ. Press, 1967.

Shaffer, R. *Keys to Genera of Higher Fungi*. 2nd ed. Ann Arbor: Univ of Michigan Biol. Station, 1968.

Singer, R. *Agaricales in Modern Taxonomy*. 3rd ed., rev. Weinheim: J. Kramer, 1975.

Smith, A. *Mushrooms in Their Natural Habitat*. Portland: Sawyer's, 1949.

Snell, W. and Dick, E. *A Glossary of Mycology*. Cambridge: Harvard Univ. Press, 1957.

Toxicology

Benedict, R. "Killer Mushrooms". *Pacific Search*, May 1972.

Bodin, F. and Cheinisse, C. *Poisons*. London: World University Library, 1957.

Buck, R. "Psychedelic Effects of *Pholiota spectabilis*". *The New England Journal of Medicine* 276:1964.

Buck, R. "Poisoning by Wild Mushrooms". *Clinical Medicine* 71:1964.

Catalfomo, P. and Eugster. "*Amanita muscaria*: Present Understanding of its Chemistry". *Bulletin on Narcotics* 22:1970.

Fiume, L. "Mechanism of Action of Phalloidin". *Lancet* 1:1975.

Floersheim, G. "Curative Potencies against Amanitin Poisoning by Cytochrome c.". *Science* 177:1972.

Genest, K. et al. "Potentiation of ethanol by *Coprinus atramentarius* in Mice". *Journal of Pharmacy* 20:1968.

Harrison, D. et al. "Mushroom Poisoning in Five Patients". *American Journal of Medicine* 38:1965.

Kempton, P. and Wells, V. "Mushroom Poisoning in Alaska: Helvella". *Alaska Medicine*, March 1968.

Lampe, K. "Current Concepts of Therapy in Mushroom Intoxication". 15th Annual Meeting of the American Association of Poison Control Centers, New York, October 1972.

Laquer, U. et al. "Thiotic Acid Treatment of Acute Mushroom Poisoning". *Pennsylvania Medicine* 75:1972.

Lewandowska, E. "Fungus Poisoning in Poland in the Years 1962-1967". *Epidemiological Review* 25:1971.

Lough, J. and Kinnear, D. "Mushroom Poisoning in Canada". *Canadian Medical Association Journal* 102:1970.

Pilàt, A. *Mushrooms*. New York: Spring Books, 1957.

Ramsbottom, J. *Mushrooms and Toadstools*. London: Collins, 1954.

Reynolds, W. and Lowe, F. "Mushrooms and a Toxic Reaction to Alcohol". *New England Journal of Medicine* 272:1965.

Simons, D. "The Mushroom Toxins". *De-laware Medical Journal* 43:1971.

Stolman, A. *Progress in Chemical Toxicology*. New York: Academic Press, 1963.

Taber, C. *Taber's Cyclopedic Medical Dictionary*. 11th ed., Philadelphia: F.A. Davis, 1970.

Tyler, V. "Poisonous Mushrooms". *Progress in Chemical Toxicology* 1:1963.

Vella, E. and Macfie, W. "Mushroom Poisoning". *Journal of the Royal Army Medical Corps* 110:1964.

Weingart, J. "Mushroom Poisoning". Seminar, The Faculty of the Mayo Graduate School of Medicine, 1967.

Ethnomycology

Allegro, J. *The Sacred Mushroom and the Cross*. Garden City and New York: Doubleday, 1970.

Hofmann, A. "Teonanàcatl and Ololiuqui, two ancient magic drugs of Mexico". *Bulletin on Narcotics* 23:1971.

Wasson, V. and Wassom, R. *Mushrooms, Russia and History*. New York: Pantheon, 1957.

Wasson, R. *Soma. Divine Mushroom of Immortality*. New York: Harcourt, Brace and World, 1968.

Recommended Reading

Harris, Bob. *Growing Wild Mushrooms*. Berkeley: Wingbow Press, 1979.

Heim, R. and Wasson, R. *Les Champignons Hallucinogènes du Mexique*. Paris: Musée National d'Histoire Naturelle, 1958.

Lilly, J. *The Center of the Cyclone*. New York: Julian Press, 1972.

Stamets, Paul. *Psilocybe Mushrooms and Their Allies*. Seattle: Homestead Book Company, 1978.

Index

Genera and Species

Toxins